THE PATRIOT INN

THE INNKEEPERS GUIDE

ELLA VERLE AND RONALD D. WEISS

ROYAL CROWN
PUBLISHING

THE INNKEEPERS
&
AUTHORS:

Ella Verle and Ronald D. Weiss

FORWARD

The Innkeepers' Guide gives the potential innkeeper a complete knowledge of owning and managing an inn-B&B. It takes the reader from *how to* manage the smallest details of business to *how to* market and promote it.

Ella Verle Weiss opens her secret recipe files and shares with you the favorite foods loved by their clientele. B&B's magazines have featured Verle's recipes.

The twelve and a half years of a very successfully managed B&B business makes innkeepers Verle and Ron Weiss excellent resources. Their commonsense approach to the realities of running a B&B makes this book a valuable tool.

Follow their helpful suggestions and you will hear, "Thank you for refreshing us! Our visit at The Patriot Inn was simply wonderful. You both have a wonderful gift for making others feel at home."

This book also includes inspiring stories from The Patriot Inn's beginnings. These experiences create a rich tapestry of history woven into The Patriot Inn. You may experience similar stories if you choose to become an innkeeper.

This book is not only an enjoyable read, but a detailed guide on successfully managing a Bed and Breakfast.

DEDICATION:

To immediate, extended, and Bed & Breakfast families.
To Patriots who have, and continue to keep our country safe
To Marquis de La Fayette

Ella Verle Weiss

Ella Verle Weiss stands by her painting La Fayette. Verle has done extensive research on Marquis de La Fayette. Her favorite reference material was by Harlow Giles Unger. Ron and Verle made a rare visit to the estate where the Marquis spent his last years, The Chateau de La Grange, located on the edge of Brie, France.

MARQUIS DE LA FAYETTE

By Ella Verle Weiss

We must always remember the Marquis de La Fayette, or *Lafayette*. He always used *Lafayette* as his signature when writing to his superior officers.

He gave his fortunes to the Colonial Revolutionists to make America a free country. He purchased military uniforms and equipped the Revolutionary troops with combat gear. Lafayette went back to France different times for more financial and military support from the French Government.

Lafayette became like a son to George Washington. The Marquis named his only son George Washington La Fayette, and his youngest daughter Virginie after the Commonwealth Of Virginia.

Yorktown, Virginia has a wonderful National Park Museum and statue dedicated to the America Revolution. The museum spotlights Lafayette for his wonderful contributions to America.

On October 27, 1824 Lafayette returned to Portsmouth as an honored guest. A short distance from The Patriot Inn there is a park with an arch dedicated to his honor. There is a plaque commemorating La fayette's visit in front of the Towne Bank.

THE PATRIOT INN
By Ella Verle Weiss

The Patriot Inn is an architectural gem built in 1784, located in the Olde Towne Portsmouth National Historic District. The busy Elizabeth River waterfront is reflected in the hand blown window panes, just as it has been for over 200 years. Shopping and antiquing on High Street are just a few steps away, as are the Portsmouth Naval Hospital, the Tidewater Yacht Marina, and Norfolk waterside ferry.

This Colonial, English half-basement with Federal influence, rests on foundations of another dwelling dating to 1772. According to official documents, Thorowgood Keeling, a first lieutenant in the Virginia Milita, built the current dwelling in 1784. The earliest known owner of this property was Reverend John Agnew, a Tory Chaplain, who was a colonist loyal to King George III.

The American Revolutionary War played an important role in molding the history of Olde Towne Portsmouth. General Cornwallis, whose headquarters were in Olde Towne Portsmouth, decided to relocate his troops to Yorktown and loaded them on boats in front of the Patriot Inn. During this time, General Charles Lee was in charge of the forces that burned this Tory home to the foundation as an example to colonists still loyal to the king.

The Patriot Inn has been owned by many people in the history of Portsmouth. Nathaniel Pead, a shoe merchant, owned the home from 1787 to 1827. Other noteworthy owners were: Claudis W. Murdaugh, judge of the Court of Hustings; John H. Gayle, a member of the State Legislature, and Aurthur Emmerson, clerk of the Court of Hustings.

As the exterior of the home reflects colonial architectural details, the interior is discreetly decorated offering interesting corners to relax and enjoy the tranquility that permeates this lovely old Inn. With the original heart of pine wood floors, the stately main staircase, and the wonderfully carved mantles, the Inn is filled with furnishings that enable guests to step back in time and experience the spirit of colonial America.

Note: This is the inside of The Patriot Inn brochure shown in the appendix.

CONTENTS:

ACKNOWLEDGMENTS:

Ron and I give special thanks to Vivien Willis. She provided encouragement and enduring assistance while embracing and assembling this book. We are eternally grateful to her. Her steady persistence kept us on task and focused.

A very special thank you goes to my wonderful mentor and author of the book *Lafayette*, Harlow Giles Unger. In it he reveals the authentic character of Lafayette. He is the author of eight books on American Education and lives in New York City and Paris, France.

DESTINY AWAITS: THE PATRIOT INN
By Ella Verle Weiss

Our whole adventure or misadventure of owning and managing an inn was inconceivable for Ron and me. We were full-time assistant professors of biology at Iowa Western Community College, Council Bluffs, Iowa. We owned a lake home on Lake Manawa in a National Wildlife Preserve. Ron and I were content with our life, and really were not ready for early retirement from our teaching positions.

However, our son Denton and daughter-in-law, Michelle wanted us to move to Virginia. They wanted us to move close enough for Ron and I to have more time with their two daughters, Micaela and Natasha. Denton is a successful plastic surgeon. He is internationally known. He and his wife Michelle have established themselves as pillars in the community and have contributed to many charitable causes.

Our granddaughter Natasha discovered the house which is now The Patriot Inn. She was walking down the street in front of the picturesque old house.

She exclaimed "This is the bed and breakfast for Grandpa and Grandma!" The *old rooming house* became an inspiration for our further investigation. We called Denton and said we would consider it. We explained, "An engineer needs to check the foundation and other facets of the building."

Now Denton, Michelle, Micaela and Natasha were leaving for Rota, Spain. Denton would be performing surgery there for 2 months. This left us with no contacts except Denton's friend Donald Dixon. Don lived across the street from this *run down* rooming house.

Don had agreed he would hire a person to inspect the house to make sure the house was stable. The inspector also had to check if we could renovate the property, and still keep it's colonial character.

Our phone calls were many, and we managed to get the details. Denton arrived back in the states with his family in time to sign the legal house papers. We arrived later on June 1, 2000 with three loads of furniture.

It had been a long trek with large rental trucks and our van. Our dear friends Gene, Shirley, Duane and Kristy Zenk helped us drive the long trip to Portsmouth. We crossed Iowa, Illinois, Indiana,Kentucky, and through the mountains of Virginia which was quite challenging at times.

Previous to moving there, we had flown to Virginia to look at the proposed house. I saw the inside of house and retorted, "They should burn the damn place down!" However, the winds of the North Easterly crept into our hearts. We began to consider becoming part of Virginia.

Portsmouth is a peaceful beautiful place to live. We remembered that the most important element for being a successful B&B was *location, location, location!* The location of The Patriot Inn was and is perfect. We love being on the Elizabeth River across from Norfolk Virginia which has a pedestrian ferry that runs every half hour. That is just one of many activities that guests can do here.

It is one of the best kept secrets in Hampton Roads. It is a lovely old port city which really never got the recognition it deserved. Portsmouth's history has been almost hidden along with its river views. The largest naval base in the world is about five miles north of us, in the Chesapeake Bay. The Norfolk shipyard is in Portsmouth Bay, just a few street blocks south from our Inn. The Joint Forces Command is about 15 minutes from the Inn.

This was no *turn-key* project we were considering (twelve plus years ago). Yet we decided to go ahead with it. The whole house restoration was a community project starting on June 3rd, 2000. Friendships with locals developed immediately. They started to help when we became too exhausted to go on.

Some primed the whole house inside with paint. The following people painted:Don and Ron Dixon, Jeanne and John Larcombe, Doris and Roney Leitner, Claire Marie Fisther-Oleary, Rob and Susan Hansen, and Grace Taylor Hansen, Denton, Michelle, Micaela, and Natasha Weiss, Tim Lyke and Katherine Schuhr, Mark and Ulla Geduldig Yatrofsky, Mark and Cheryl Woodland, Alan Gollihue and Lane Killam Gollihue.

Denton and Michelle and their two daughters generously opened their home to us for five and a half months. Finally, we moved into one finished bedroom and bath. We named it the Lee bedchamber after the notorious General Charles Lee.

Lee challenged George Washington continually during the revolutionary war. He traveled down the Elizabeth River with his revolutionists and destroyed the homes of the Tories in Portsmouth. That included The Patriot Inn's first structure. It burned between 1775-1776 only the 1772 foundation remained as it remains today. We still possess the documents which signify the truth of the home's origin. Reverend John Agnew was the original owner.

Ron and I found living in one bedroom and bath difficult. We purchased a small table from Yvonne Lerner, the owner of Alden's Antiques. Yvonne had brought the table from England. It was a tiger-leg maple with drop leaves It was incredulous that we would sit at that table and feast on fast foods. Imagine using plastic plates, flatware, and paper napkins as well. Indeed, how we compromised that table's dignity! This was the first of many English antiques we purchased from Alden's Antiques.

In the Agnew bathroom the floor was in total disrepair. The only thing holding the stool up was the drain pipe under the stool. Denton and Michelle had promised to fix it on a weekend. A Polish Priest. Father Piotr Tarnawski arrived at Portsmouth to stay with them for a week. It worked out well because the priest said "I would enjoy helping you. I was a carpenter before I became a priest." They completely renovated the floor. It was like new.

Father Piotr Tarnawski, Denton and Michelle Weiss working on Inn.

Yes, indeed, those were the days we reminisce about, but would not want to live over. It is a beautiful peaceful May evening here in Portsmouth. I am sitting here on the veranda, drinking a glass of sparkling pink lemonade, and contemplating how lovely our Inn had become. We had the best of all guests. Many military couples became like family.

The officers who came from Los Alamos Laboratory in New Mexico always intrigued us. Every guest had a special story of his own. Frankly, too many stories to record in a book. They will each remain a memory stored, sometimes a mystery still unfolded in our hearts.

DR. DENTON D. WEISS FAMILY:

Above: Dr. Denton and Michelle Weiss (wife), Micaela and Thomas Singer, Natasha and Matthew Huff, and below:

Helaina Singer

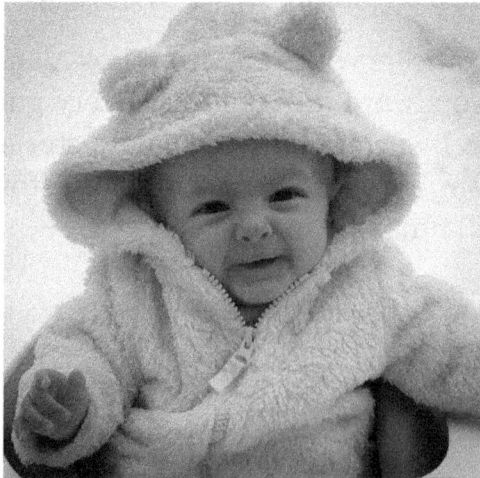

6

2

ON THE PRACTICAL SIDE:

By Ronald D. Weiss

Don Dixon who had restored the Grice-Neeley house across the street from us was a big help when we renovated our home. He also knew the rules about getting permits for a B&B. He reminded us to get at least three bids on every project. The bids will vary. This saved us thousands of dollars.

Our first task was to take down the plaster off the walls. We also took down the wall that divided the main hall, making the hall beautiful and spacious. A demolition company we hired hauled off 37 truck loads from the property. Ken Struthers bid much lower then the other two bidders, so we hired him and his crew. I was happy because I knew Ken would do a good job of it.

Mike King was a *master plasterer*. We were so fortunate to have him plaster all the rooms including the medallions and some of the crown molding. Mike was an excellent artisan. Our son, Dr. Denton Weiss made a tool for Mike so Mike could imprint the initial K for *King* inside the medallions.

The electricity, heating, and cooling units were done by Brooks Electric. Mike Balser did baseboards and other woodworking in the 1870 addition of the inn. He electrified and assembled all the 36 wall sconces.

Ron Herrick, a carpenter handmade 16 windows to replace those boarded up and in ill repair. We placed insulation in the inside walls, outside walls and in some ceilings before plastering. This was done by the Smith family. When you own an inn you need to have a handy-man that can do many different jobs at a reasonable price. You have no time to do repairs when you are busy with guests.

Two brick masons came and restored and re-pointed six fireplaces. A chimney sweep followed the restoration. Fireplaces are now in operation. While the inside walls of the Inn were down, a gas contractor ran gas lines to all of the fireplaces.

Ralph Orsi is a full-time psychologist at Omaha, Nebraska. He was our lab assistant at the Iowa Western Community College. Ralph flew in to Portsmouth-Norfolk a good number of times to do the woodworking on the Inn. He built the stringer which now supports the grand staircase.

Ralph continues to come and work on our crown moldings or other woodwork projects.

Keith Maas, a corpsman for Dr. Denton Weiss at Portsmouth Naval Hospital worked any spare hour on tiling our bathrooms. He acted as my right hand man. We would review the days work and try to tie up any loose ends for the day.

Keith spent our first Christmas with us in the Lee bedchamber, as that was the only finished room in the house.

8

Keith brought a poinsettia for our little table and we ate Chinese food. Thanks for the memories!

Our main painters were Lloyd *Skinny* Saunders and Paul Saunders. They were invaluable painters.

Innkeeper Ronald D. Weiss was the contractor who acquired all the bids from a number of sub contractors. From that group, he chose the contractor who did quality work for the least amount of money.

Ralph Orsi

"The dirt from the soldiers boots

sifted down through the cracks

of the pine boards

to the basement below."

3

THE OLD ROOMING HOUSE RENAMED
By Ella Verle Weiss

One day David suggested we go see the movie *The Patriot* by Mel Gibson and think about calling our B&B *The Patriot Inn.*He said that the houses featured in the movie had the same *feel* as ours. The movie was showing at the Commodore theater which is a few blocks from the Inn. Ron and I went to see it.

THE PATRIOT INN

The movie definitely influenced our decision. We saw the connection between the movie's history and the history of our B&B. We saw other characteristics that held true to our own house. If you saw the movie, you might remember the scene where the people were hiding in the lower level from the British soldiers. The dirt from the soldiers boots sifted down through the cracks of the pine boards to the basement below. That reminded us of the heart of pine boards that we have at the Inn.

Ron and I called David back, after going back the second time to see the movie, and said it was the perfect name. We had the name copyrighted and patented; thus The Patriot Inn became a reality.

Incidentally, we purchased the movie after it came out on the market. We watch the movie now and then. It reminds us of where we began on this road of restoration. We like many others in this historic district have saved our property's legacy. We are caretakers of Portsmouth's history itself.

Artist David M. Weiss

THE OLD ROOMING HOUSE RENAMED

VIEW FROM THE PATRIOT INN

Photographer: Ella Verle Weiss

"I am sitting here on the veranda,

drinking a glass of sparkling pink lemonade,

contemplating

how lovely our inn had become.

We had the best of all guests.

Many military couples became like family."

4

THE ROOMING HOUSE
By Ronald D. Weiss

A man came back for a coast guard reunion. He told us that four of his Coast Guard friends had stayed at The Patriot Inn. His friends and he were working for the Coast Guard Administration.

That office remains in Olde Town Portsmouth near the post office. At that time The Patriot Inn was a rooming house. The rooming house gave the coast guard members meals as part of their stay. It was probably the first time it was like a B&B, but did not have the name, The Patriot Inn.

Innkeeper Ronald D. Weiss

RON TAKING TIME OUT FOR GUESTS.

5

THE INN'S BEDCHAMBERS
By Ronald D. Weiss

The Inn has all the bedchambers on the second floor with the stairs going two different directions after the first landing. Our suite is on the third floor. It is unique with open beams and a railing that matches that of the stately main staircase. The east windows face the Elizabeth River. We could look down North Street from the west windows. They also give us a beautiful tranquil view which is characteristic of this beautiful port city called Portsmouth.

The Patriot Inn had four bedchambers for guests. Verle and I had given each of them a name. We called one the Lee bedchamber for General Charles Lee. He was a colonel in the Revolutionary Militia. He brought his forces to Portsmouth about 1775-1776. Though he was a rough leader the army needed Generals, so George Washington commissioned him.

We named one bedchamber the Dale bedchamber, after Commodore Dale. He lived during the same era of the above mentioned men. He was in charge of the Naval

Gosport Shipyard in Portsmouth. Officially the Gosport Shipyard changed to Norfolk Naval Shipyard. This surprised us because it still occupies Portsmouth, Virginia.

Of course, we named one the Marquis de La Fayette bedchamber because he helped win the Revolutionary War.

AGNEW BEDCHAMBER

The house that sat on our original foundation burned to the ground by Lee's command. Reverend John Agnew and his family owned the house. The Agnew family was loyal to the King of England. They were Tories and enemies to America. Because the Agnews were the original owners of the location,we named one bedchamber after the Reverend.

The Lee bedchamber, the Agnew bedchamber, the Lafayette bedchamber, and the Dale bedchamber stood as reminders of the days gone past.

6

DESIGNING THE ROOMS
By Ella Verle Weiss

Dana our daughter is a licensed interior designer. She and her family lived in Houston, Texas at the time we moved to Virginia. Four different times she flew to Virginia, and stayed with us for two weeks to help me design the Inn. We were both perfectionists at bringing together beauty, function, and authenticity. We supervised every detail of the restoration.

We visited Mt. Vernon, George Washington's home to authenticate our design ideas. It was typical of our inn's time frame. We replicated the style they used for their steps to build ours going to our third floor suite. At Monticello, we looked at draperies, furniture, and accessories. We also studied the life style and history of the 18th century.

Before Ron and I moved to Virginia, we had a home built in Denison, Iowa. We ordered Virginia style blueprints from the Colonial Home Magazine which my sister, Vivien had shown me. We lived there for 24 years. So, we already had many period furniture pieces and furniture reproductions that fit into the Inn's new image. We have continued to add many authentic pieces from the 18th and 19th centuries since the Inn's beginning. I still have stacks of *Colonial Home's* magazine which inspired most of our design work for the Inn.

We kept paint samples on file at the local Pittsburgh Paint center. We chose colors appropriate for the era of the original property.

Ron and I had visited the Wayside Inn in Massachusetts when Denton was at Harvard. Denton's family, Ron, and I went there for dinner one evening. I fell in love with the ambiance of the lighting they had. The Wayside Inn had arranged the candle lights in sconces all down the halls. They were breathtakingly beautiful. I wanted to reproduce that look.

Dana and I went to Williamsburg for parts to make the wall sconces. My daughter in law Michelle Weiss ordered other parts. The three of us, Dana, Michelle, and I designed them. Michael Balser wired them. Now you can look down the halls and experience the enchantment of them. They are magical.

We have thirty-seven candle lights in the windows and a single switch turns them on. We added a timer so the candle lights would turn on automatically at five o'clock in the evening. They shut off at eleven o'clock at night. Above all the fireplaces we put spot lights in the ceilings which light the oil paintings below.

Lighting is so important, and there were no lighting fixtures in the house when we purchased it.

Interior Designer Dana Weiss Petersen in the Library

We looked for just the right lighting fixtures. Carravatis was a salvage company located in Richmond, Virginia. They rescued items including lighting fixtures from historic buildings. One of their salvaged sites was Warner Hall near Gloucester,Virginia. We purchased items removed from there.

On one of our many trips we found that they had just brought in a brass chandelier from there. We immediately bought it. Michelle and I cleaned it, and hung it in the parlour.

Our son David is a professional cinematographer, fine arts , and commercial artist. Tracy, his wife, is a RN at the Methodist Woman's Hospital at Omaha, Nebraska. David *designed our logo*. We proudly display his art throughout the inn. An upcoming movie features his artwork.

THE DAVID M. WEISS FAMILY

Grant, David, Tracy(wife),Chelsie, and dog-Romey

DESIGNING THE ROOMS

Painting by Artist David M. Weiss

David is a professional artist whose work is prized by well respected galleries. He has also been featured in an International Artist Magazine. Check out his other beautiful paintings on his website www.dmweiss.com.

Painting by Artist David M. Weiss

Painting by Artist David M. Weiss

Painting by Artist David M. Weiss

The Library

Painting above fireplace by Artist David M. Weiss

Painting by Artist David M. Weiss

TABLE IN THE PARLOUR

Painting above the table is by Artist Ella Verle Weiss

THE SMALL COURTYARD

Photographer: Ella Verle Weiss

Susan Heely In The Parlour

Painting above fireplace by Artist Vivien Whitewolf Willis

FORMAL DINING ROOM PLACE SETTINGS FOR GUESTS

Painting above fireplace by Artist Vivien Whitewolf Willis

7

SET UP YOUR BUSINESS

By Ella Verle Weiss

1 Hire an accountant who has worked with other B&Bs or inns.We used James E. Hoffmeister, CPA.

2. Acquire a business license downtown City Hall.

3. City parking permits are required for guests.

4. Acquire a credit card machine, but be wary of some businesses who offer this service. It can be costly. Watch out for scams. Some Inns only take cash/checks.

5. Apply for a copyright for your business' name at local City Hall.

6. List your business hours.

7. You will need to take a food handling course and pass the test required by the local Health Department.

8. Each year the Health Department thoroughly inspects your Bed & Breakfast.

9. You are required by the Federal Government and the State of Virginia to display regulation notices affecting your employees. They update labor law notices on a regular basis. Check your state.

8

MARKETING
By Ella Verle Weiss

You have to consider all the pros and cons of your marketing strategies. We used many strategies to draw attention to our inn. We allowed photo shoots free for students. We allowed the Regent University of Virginia Beach to use our Inn as their drama stage. They did a production of *The Tell-Tale Heart*, by Edgar Allen Poe.

Michelle Harrel and her husband had a photo shoot for advertizing the local *Ghost Walk*. The Portsmouth Civic League sponsors it every year. They photographed her coming down the stairs in her white wedding gown as *the lady in white*. The *Ghost Walk* commemorates *the lady in white* who supposedly ran from the house to the river to drown herself. She was so distraught about her husband's military death.

Our top marketing tools were B&B websites. They included: bbonline.com, bedandbreakfast.com, and Bed & Breakfast association of Virginia. Use Google, trip advisor, yelp, the local business associations periodical, face-book, and others for advertisements. At one time we were on 48 sites of exposure due to our guests writing about us.

You will need a hard copy daily planner like we had. You will also need similar forms like what we used when people called in for a reservation. If clients reserved on line, we hard copied their reservation. Then we placed it in the pages of the planner for that particular month.

You must have a brochure and a business card. Examples of these are given in the appendix of this book. Always carry a business card. Both brochures and business cards are a source of advertisement, and should be kept available for guests. If there is a visitor's center, be sure to put your brochures there.

Innkeepers need to join local business associations. The Chamber of Commerce and Civic League are usually available.

Community activities completely immersed us. We gave nights and weekend reservations as silent auction items, for example, the Portsmouth Museums Foundation Gala. The Florida and Pennsylvania National Public Radio had a silent auction to raise money. We donated a weekend reservation to them. We made donations to schools also.The Inn participated in the local Olde Towne Holiday Home Tour two times, the Holly Home Tour, and the Virginia Garden Tour. We held a reception for the Todi Music Festival, and parties for the neighborhood after the tours. These were all provided by us free, which was good exposure for the Inn!

We allowed showers and wedding rehearsal dinners, for example: Janice Cuneo and her husband David. The family stayed in the Inn as paying guests.

The Washington Post 3-31-2008, and Hampton Roads Magazine featured The Patriot Inn in their periodicals. HGTV Restore America selected and featured The Patriot Inn in April 2004. Dan Schmit and David Reitz gave their time and effort to make it happen.

Our granddaughter Britni Petersen worked holidays and summers at The Patriot Inn. She kept descriptions and changes current for the online promotions on sites we mentioned above. She entertained guests when time allowed by talking about the historic features of the Inn, and would give them a tour explaining the architectural features. After graduating from George Mason University in Fairfax, Virginia, she is now the Editor of the Washington D.C Family Magazine.

Britni Petersen

Our granddaughter Brooke Petersen helped us occasionally with baking, and picked up information off the internet for us. She did this between attending high school and college. Now she is a sophomore at Old Dominion University in Norfolk, Virginia.

James D. Petersen our son-in-law and an Esquire of Lexis-Nexis was and continues to be an invaluable help. He helps us with legal matters and constantly works on our computer. You must get legal advice on all elements of business including marketing.

THE JAMES D. PETERSEN FAMILY:

Dana Weiss Petersen and James D. Petersen

Britni and Brooke Petersen

THE BENJAMIN KERR FAMILY:

Ashley Petersen Kerr, Benjamin Kerr,
Baby Abigail, Ethan, and Noah

THE WILLIAM SMITH FAMILY :

Nicole Petersen Smith, William Smith, and Baby Addison

9

THE PATRIOT INN PROTOCOL
By Ella Verle Weiss

A. *Keys:*

1. We had two sets of keys for each room, which included a room key and front entrance key. We used colored plastic stretch key chains that pull over the hand. We used red for the Lee, green for the Lafayette, violet for the Agnew and blue for the Commodore Dale bedchamber.

2. Besides having two sets for guests we also had a back up set of the original keys. We kept them in a separate location, so they could be reproduced.

3. We used Tweeds Key Makers and purchased a lock on the front door that could be changed as we could make a different key in case our guests lost theirs. We changed the keys approximately six times from the beginning to the end time of our business.

4. We kept a code for the colors and keys in a side table by the front door where they were easily accessed as the guests arrived. When they arrived they were given a set of keys, a parking pass, a brochure, and a business card with our cell numbers. They could contact us at any time as we were on call 24/7.

B. *Bedchamber standard items:*

1. Free computer access was available.

2. A battery driven alarm clock was in each room.

3. Bibles were placed in each room.

4. Free cable television was available.

5. Dishes were placed in every room for candy and mints. (We had a large container in the closet to keep them available for refill.)

6. Do not clutter your inn with things you have collected through the years. People are there to relax not hear about or see your great collections. Leave space for your guests to put things in their rooms, for example tables free of clutter. Also provide luggage rack, armoires, closets, or coat stands to hang clothing.

7. All rooms had smoke detectors. Fire extinguishers were placed throughout the Inn for easy access. (We could not have candles in the rooms due to fire hazards, and being purists, we did not want the artificial ones.)

8. A fire escape diagram was placed on each and every bedchamber door.

9. Compressed logs were used in the Inns fireplaces. They would burn for 2 ½ hours.

10. Throws were put on wing chairs near the fireplaces for guest's warmth.

11. Beverage coasters were placed in each bedchamber.

12. Stands were located on both sides of the bed for lamps.

13. We used white paper lace doilies under the drinking glasses. We purchased them at the Dollar General Store.

14 Every bedchamber window had blackout shades.

15. Shutters covered the lower half of the windows.

16. All linen including curtains were white, so they could be bleached with Clorox.

C. *Bedchamber linens:*

1. All pillows and mattresses were encased in plastic and zippered closed to prevent stains, dust, and germs.

2. We assembled on the bed, the mattress pad, bottom sheet, top sheet, and the matelasse'(a flat quilted comforter). The duvet is folded at the bottom of the bed. We folded the top sheet down over the folded back matelasse'.We had four pillows which had pillow cases and pillow covers zipped on. The pillows were placed upright rather than laying flat.

3. All top sheets were ironed with water and steam only. Do not use fabric softener of spray on starch on linens as it breaks down fibers.

4. We ironed the top 24" of the sheets which allowed the turn-back. The pillow cases were also ironed.

5. Decorator pillows and European pillows were added for ambiance.

6.We had two sets of pillows and duvets that were either

feather filled or fiber filled as some people are allergic to feathers.

7. Tide was used for all of our linens which were white: sheets, pillow cases, mattress covers, coverlet, and anything else that could be bleached. I used Splashless Clorox on tough stains. Shout was used for all stains including wine if it was sprayed soon after material was stained. When one of our guest's fiance' put roses on the bed for their wedding night, the roses stained the sheets. My daughter in-law, Michelle suggested we soak them overnight in a Clorox plus Cascade mixture. It worked great! The stain was gone.

8. Bedchambers had to be turned over immediately after the guests left. I often thought of *what* our military people told us, especially the submariners on the sub marines who did what they called *hot bedding*. One jumped out leaving the bed warm, and another jumped in as they changed shifts.

9. The Inn had 38 steps up and 38 steps down the staircase. At night we took baskets of linens and laundry or needed items with us up the steps. And after we cleaned the empty rooms we took soiled linens down in the baskets. We had two baskets for transporting items.

10. Writing stationary was available in each bedchamber chest of drawers.

D. *Bedchamber bathrooms:*

1. Cleaning agents were purchased from the local Dollar General when they had the product. For cleaning stools we used Comet and a stool brush, then wiped the whole stool down with Clorox wipes.

2. We used Lysol spray for sinks, bath tubs and bidets.

We purchased concentrated Lysol and diluted it down, and put it in plastic spray bottles. This is what we had used in our bio labs at college and found it very effective.

3. We used Guardsman furniture polish from Bed, Bath & Beyond. Another good cleaner is Amazing found at the Dollar Tree for stubborn stains. For mirrors and glass we used Sprayway glass cleaner as it is ammonia free from Lowes Hardware.

4. All of our inner shower curtains were from Restoration Hardware made of a tight woven nylon instead of distasteful plastic. They could be bleached.

5. The health department demands every bathroom have lids on their wastebaskets. We chose woven baskets, with plastic lining and lids, from Longaberger Baskets of Pennsylvania.

6. Each bathroom had shampoo, moisturizer, hand lotion, and hand soap in dispenser bottles with pewter labels.

7. We also had personalized soaps. Our logo was a sketch of the Inn drawn and designed by our son, David Weiss. We sent the logo to Greenwich Bay Trading Co. P.O. Box 90787, Raleigh, NC 27675-0787. Telephone 800-323-1209 customerservice@gbsoaps.com. They printed the soap with the logo. They are an incredible company and I still get our personal soap from them.

8. Four rolled bath towels, four rolled hand towels, and four wash cloths were put in each bedchamber bathroom. We also had terry cloth bath rugs and nonslip bathmats that were soft, flexible, and washable.

9. We folded the end of toilet tissues into a V point and secured it to the roll with a Patriot Inn seal.

10. Every bathroom had a small bathroom night light.

E. *Other Perks for Guests:*

1. Hall closet: We had one microwave and one refrigerator in a hall closet that provided our guests with free sodas and bottles of water. They often put food brought back from a restaurant or extra food they could store there.

2. Umbrellas: five umbrellas were always available for guests to use on rainy or hot sunny days.

F. *More B&B Tips:*

1. Be sure and have a high liability insurance for guests and staff. Note: stairways can be a real hazard and especially with carpeting which might have a fringe. Be sure that people can walk free of obstacles in your B&B. The old saying, "An ounce of prevention is worth a pound of cure"is true. Walk through your Inn and look for any accidents waiting to happen. We chose Farm Bureau because it was one third the cost of other policies.

2. We did not have children under 12 years of age because of all the steps we had and the open staircases. Many of our guests came to relax and enjoy their vacation. When children are running through the house, no one can relax.

3. We did not have dogs or cats, as many people are allergic to animals. We love children and animals, but they do not always work for guests.

4. Magazines, maps, brochures, local information about historical sites within 50 miles radius of your B&B were laid out on tables, convenient for guests. Local picture postcards were made available, free as well.

5. We had chalk and chalkboard for messages to guests.

6.Choose quality grocers, such as Sam's Club and Restaurant Depot, if they are available. Basic staples can be purchased at a grocery store close by. For quality and the unusual, I often traveled farther to Trader Joes, especially for cheese.

7. We used Farberware coffee percolators to make our coffee, regular and decaf. We sprinkled ½ teaspoon of cinnamon on top of the coffee grounds before perking

8. We had a complete security system installed through JOHNSBROTHERS security which was only used while Ron and I were alone. We had it shut down because we had so many people coming and going it set off the motion detectors.

9. *Post its* were important for notes left on the doors. Messages were left for a guest leaving early, to tell them thank you and goodbye.

10. We had a small courtyard garden in the back to supply herbs that we used in our food preparation. This was very handy during the warm months.

11. Choose good friends you can trust to be inn-sitt Some other B&B owners from other areas like to trade places. They could be inn-sitters for you and you could sit for their B&B for a change of scenery. We never did that, but we did have available offers.

12. Purchase receipt books for paying guests at Wal Mart.

13. Always greet guests, and greet them with a friendly smile.

14. There were four common rooms where guests could congregate: dining, library, parlour, and the lowest level *man cave*.

15. Constant maintenance of house and grounds was a must. Bids were important for repairs. We had a *handyman* list near the telephone.

16. Guests were allowed to come to the door of the kitchen during breakfast preparations.

17. Only a few guests chose the option of breakfast in their rooms. They came downstairs, and took it to their rooms.

18. We still have a commercial stove,convection oven, two refrigerators, a freezer, and a dishwasher.

19. An 85 gallon hot water heater was necessary for four bedchambers. They all had showers in their bathrooms.

20. Multicolored place-mats were used in place of tablecloths in the dining room.

21. A washer and dryer was available for guests.

10

AFTERNOON WINE
By Ella Verle Weiss

We served Afternoon wine at 5:00. We chose Williamsburg Governors White and Beringer Cabernet Sauvignon Red. These wines were served with trays of different cheeses, fruit, crackers, sometimes cold cuts, fruits, meats, and pate'.Occasionally people wanted tea and dessert.

WINE, CHEESE AND CRACKERS-SERVED IN THE PARLOUR

11

BREAKFAST AT THE PATRIOT INN
By Ella Verle Weiss

MENU:

1. BEVERAGES: Regular and decaf coffee were made in a percolator. Put 1/2 teaspoon cinnamon in coffee grounds prior to percolating. Assorted teas, water, milk cold, warmed, or hot chocolate.

2. FRUIT: We served fresh fruit in season. In the winter we served Del Monte fruit, canned in glass jars, and mixed with fresh apples, bananas, and/or blueberries. We served them in a stemmed sherbet dish.

3. MEATS: Ham steak, sausage, bacon,or Polish Kiebalsa sausage were served. Bacon was fried/baked in oven on a Pampered Chef stone ware bar pan at 375°.

4. EGGS: Scrambled, poached, baked,quiche,omelet, fried eggs, or in hashbrown egg casserole were breakfast choices.

5. ORANGE JUICE: We Always served it fresh in wine glasses.

6.BREADS AND CAKES: English muffins,biscuits,plain or toasted croissants, toasted multigrain bread, French toast, waffle, and crepes, scones, cinnamon rolls, toast, coffee cake, oven pancakes or muffins were guests choices.

7. CONDIMENTS: There were individual salt and pepper shakers at each setting. Butter, jams, and jellies*, heavy whipping cream, sugar, syrup, salsa, and chutneys were other choices.

EARLY BIRD RISERS: If guests wanted breakfast before 7:30 am they would have a place at the dining room table:

PLACE SETTINGS PREPARED FOR BREAKFAST

a. Hard cooked eggs were in egg cups, saran covered fresh fruit in sherbert glasses, cold cuts, and orange juice were available to them in the kitchen refrigerators.

b. Pastries or breads that they could toast were available in kitchen with a toaster.

c. Orange juice could be poured into their wine glasses placed on table.

d. The guests had a selection of teas in a tea caddy. Coffee was in perculator ready to be plugged in by guests.

e. Sugar and cream were set on the table. Butter patties and jams were also put there. Guests who wanted to eat early helped themselves.

12

OUR FIRST PAYING GUESTS
By Ronald D. Weiss

Dean and Peggy Burgess asked me one day when we were going to open the Inn. Peggy said their daughter was getting married and Dean's sister would take all four rooms if we were open. My response was "We will be open."

Kathie Jo and Bob Allen

51

After making that statement Verle and I decided we would have Kathie Jo Allen, Verle's niece, and her husband Bob Allen as as our first guests.

The Allens were from Chicago. They agreed to be our first guests and they invited their friends Irv and Dottie Lindley from Manhattan, New York. The four of them had all been reps of clothing companies. They had traveled much so we wanted them to rate the inn before we had our first paying customers. This all took place the last week in April.

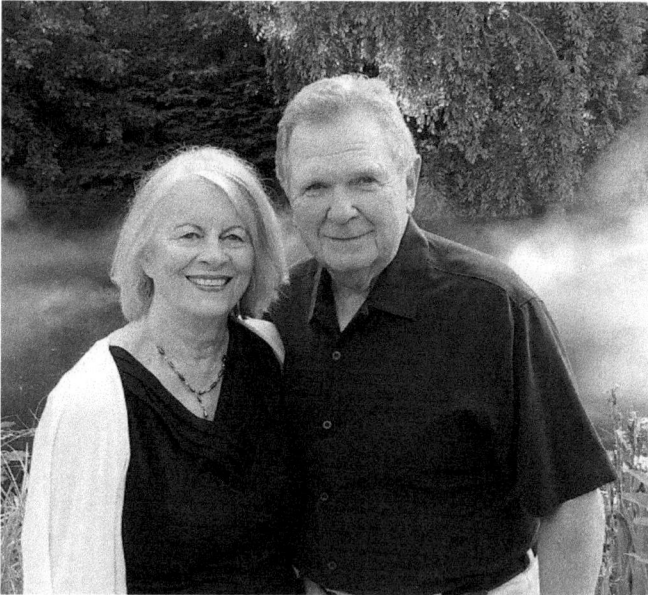

Dottie and Irv Lindley

Dean's sister and family were our first paying guest. They came for Dean and Peggy's daughter's wedding.We received the following letter from Dean Burgesses' sister:

Dear Ron and Verle, Thank you so much for your kind hospitality to me and my family. We were so proud to be your first "houseful" but am sure we will not be your last. You have a lovely establishment, and your personalities are perfect for making all feel welcome and cared for. I thought you might enjoy some pictures from our happy stay. Thank you again, and we will no doubt return one day! Warm regards from all, Diane.

May 20, 2001

Dear Ron and Verle –

Thank you so much for your kind hospitality to me and my family. We were so proud to be your first "houseful" but am sure we will not be your last. You have a lovely establishment, and your personalities are perfect for making all feel welcome and cared for. I thought you might enjoy some pictures from our happy stay. Thank you again, and we will no doubt return one day! Warm regards from all, David

13

RANDOLPH AND BISCUIT
By Ronald D. Weiss

Some interesting events occurred while we were renovating the house. I remember Randolph Booth-pharr walking his dog *Biscuit* by each day and looking in the open windows.

One day Verle said, "Come on in and bring your dog."

Randolph said,"Are you sure?" Pointing at his dog, he continued. "I have *Biscuit*! Do you allow dogs?"

Verle responded, "Are you joking, with all of this mess?"

After that he and biscuit would stop several times each week and look at the progress of renovation.

We have been friends ever since, including his new wife, Vivian of ten years. Randolph is a retired associate college professor of history, and has a doctorate in Hospital Administration and Public Health. Vivian is a High School administrator.

14

THE INN-SITTERS
By Ella Verle Weiss

We always took a three week vacation to Europe each year to be with our friends in Germany. We also visited Ron's family in France. When we left, our friends would manage the Inn.

One couple, Ruth and Richard Schnabel were often in charge. Richard had retired from the military, and Ruth was his ambitious beautiful German Bride of some years.

They both had worked in the American Embassy in Moscow and had entertained many guests. We were confident they would do an excellent job at filling in for us. Their grand daughters Hannah and Allison Halliday from Ireland and Germany also helped with inn-sitting.

We never thought or called the Inn after we boarded the plane and began our vacations. We lived and breathed for this chance of freedom. We had met Richard when he was a guest at the inn. He frequented it during a four month duration while working as a consultant. Ruth would come to stay. She became one of my dearest friends.

Our other dear friends Irvin and *Dottie* Lindley took their turn as Inn-sitters. They often helped the Schnabels when they needed it. Dottie and Irv had moved here from Manhatten, New York. They had lived in the "Big Apple" for 26 years. They were one of the two couples who came and stayed for a weekend to rate our Inn. I can still remember answering Dottie's telephone call. She asked me, "How long do you plan to live in Portsmouth?"

I told her we would probably finish our lives out here. "Why are you asking?"She told me they were thinking of moving to Portsmouth. Two years later they purchased a beautiful old home here in Portsmouth. These two couples have been invaluable for our survival these past years and a joy to us. William and Cora Lorkiewicz also participated in Inn-sitting.

Richard and Ruth Schnabel

Richard and Ruth Schnabel's
Granddaughters,
Hannah & Allison Halliday

" It was such a lovely time: the girls were such a

pleasure to be around.

They would play the piano

and sing

as they worked."

Allison Halliday

15

REFLECTIONS OF OUR TIME
WITH OUR B&B FAMILY
By Laurelea Gibbs

Five years ago we were living on our sailboat, Winds Aloft. We had sailed up from the Caribbean for the summer to miss the hurricane season down in the islands. For reasons serendipitous, we chose Ocean Marine Yacht Center in Portsmouth, Va. to leave our boat for the summer.

We had lots of work to get done on the boat, as well as leave to visit our families on the West coast. We had to have the boat pulled out of the water for the work that needed to be done on it. I love to stay in Bed & Breakfasts, so I got on the internet to find one fairly close to the boat.

Casey and I went for a walk and found the Patriot Inn. We knocked on the door and were graciously welcomed by Ron & Verle to have a look around. We made a reservation for a couple of nights before we left for the West coast and for a couple of nights after we were arriving back. As things turned out, when we arrived back in Portsmouth,The work on the boat was taking longer than planned.

Long story short, we ended up staying at the Patriot Inn for 3 weeks until the boat was ready to put back into the water, During the course of that time, naturally they had other bookings, so we would move from room to room which ever one was available. There were a couple of times that it was completely booked up, so Ruth Schnabel called around to the neighbors and found room for us at Irv & Dottie Lindley's home.

During part of that time, Ron & Verle had gone to France and Ruth Schnabel and her lovely granddaughters Allison and Hannah from Ireland were taking care of the Patriot Inn. It was such a lovely time: the girls were such a pleasure to be around. They would play the piano and sing as they worked.

Every summer we would stay at the Inn while we were getting the boat ready to sail down south. We so enjoyed Ron & Verle, Richard & Ruth, Dottie and Irv, and now claim them as our Bed & Breakfast Family.

Casey and Laurilea Gibbs

16

RON IT'S BAD!
By Ronald D. Weiss

From Ron's point of view:

Andy Bongiovi was doing some handyman work at our Portsmouth Inn. One day a horrific event occurred. We were painting the roof with silver paint. Andy was using an extra long handled paint brush. He had to reach from the top of the roof to the gutters on the vintage 1784 part of the house. I was sitting in a cove on the 1870 part of the house. holding a five gallon bucket with my right knee. When I had about three gallons of paint left in the bucket, I got a cramp in my right leg. As I moved to relieve the cramp, the bucket turned sideways and spilled the paint. It hit the gutter and splashed the paint down the side of the house onto the brick sidewalk below.

Andy descended the ladder located on the other side of the house and came around to inspect the damage.

I shouted out, "Andy Check and see how bad it is!"

He hollered back, "Ron it's bad!"

We had to turn the bricks over and had to sand others.

We scraped paint off the windows and repainted the damaged part of the house.

A two day job turned into a four day job. The old saying applies here! Live and learn!

Andy is a very talented engineer graduate from East Germany. He moved from Germany to Portsmouth. Andy has citizenship in both Germany and America. He worked for STIHL in Virginia Beach for a few years. He worked part time, and helped us in many ways. He now lives in South Carolina with his wife Nannette who was originally from Norfolk, Virginia. Andy works for BMW.

Andy and Nannette Bongiovi

17

A LESSON IN GRAVITY!
By Andy Bongiovi

*Unedited and unabridged,
from Andy's perspective of "Ron it's Bad!"*

I can't remember which day it was when Ron and I met in the morning for breakfast at the Patriot Inn; but I do remember it was a cold spring day in May. It was one of those bone chilling days when you can feel every bone in your body and when you would rather have a hot tea for breakfast than coffee or cold water!

Upon driving up to the Patriot Inn, I checked out our latest project where we painted the outside of the house. It looked just perfect, with the rising sun shining on the wooden panels and the wind blowing the American flag in all directions. Ron and I worked for days to give the house a fresh coat of premium white paint. We always liked working together because we are a lot alike; except Ron is one generation older than me and his body is reminding him every day of the rule for his stage in life: if you feel pain, then you need to take it easy. I am pretty sure you know the saying about old folks being stubborn once in a while.

Ron, without a doubt, sometimes has those moments. One of those special moments I will never in my life forget and I would like to share it with you.

With stiff fingers and cold ears, I inserted the key and opened the front door of the Patriot Inn; happily anticipating my breakfast, when I realized no one was up yet. There was no sound from the coffee machine and no smell of fresh scrambled eggs hitting me as I walked through the hallway. The first thing I did was check the time on the $2.99 watch I bought just for working around the Inn. For sure, it was 8:10 am. No sign of Ron or Verle. I started making the coffee and then went back to the hallway to call up to Ron in his bedroom, "Hello, Ron! You need to come down. We have a lot of work to do today! Wake up!"

The upstairs door opened with a squeezing noise and Ron answered with a strong voice, "I will be down in a few."

It took Ron 15 minutes to come down to the kitchen. He gave me a nice warm hug and a friendly, "Good morning," as always; but I could tell from his body language that something was wrong.

"How are you,Ron? You look like you are in pain today. Are you?"

He took his glasses off and started to clean them, which means he is preparing to give a long speech. "I've got some pain in my back today," he started "and I didn't sleep well. But you bet we are going to paint the roof today. I just need to move around a little bit and I will be fine."

"Good," I said. "Then, let's start with the breakfast and we will see how you feel after wards."

Verle came to join us for breakfast and I could see she was worried. She knew he was in pain and she also knew how stubborn he can be when it comes to slowing down and moving a project to another day just to give himself a break. I was watching both of them, in between drinking my coffee and eating my wonderful eggs, when Verle started to take her glasses off. She lifted up her head and shoulder to confront Ron about his stiffness today. I instantly stopped chewing my eggs because I knew what the next 5 minutes would be. I leaned back into my chair, took a deep sip of coffee and turned my head towards Ron, who also instantly stopped chewing his breakfast. *OMG, here we go,* I thought, *it will be too funny to see how this ends.*

"Ron, do you think it is a good idea to paint the roof today? You don't feel good and I don't know if you can climb up the 11 foot ladder to paint the roof."

Ron's eyes got bigger and, I swear, if he would have still had his glasses on, they would have fogged right up in that instant! I am pretty sure his blood pressure also got a turbo boost; which always helps him to act 20 years younger.

"I don't know what you are talking about;" he retorted, "but I feel just fine this morning! I will be up in no time on the ladder and roof."

Verle looked at me with that "I think he has some screws loose today" expression and asked me if it would be all right?

I believed it was my turn to talk and said, "Don't worry, Verle. If he has issues climbing up the ladder, I will put a firecracker in his butt and shoot him up to the roof." Both of them started laughing and I was glad we all could finish breakfast without any further worries.

The longest ladder we had, I believe, was an 11 foot one, stored under the house in the crawl space and, to be honest, is always hard to get out of there. Ron and I gathered new gloves for our painting job and some painting tools. The heaviest item we had was the 10 gallon bucket filled with fresh paint; which immediately turned my head into a brainstorming highway! I had a million thoughts going through my mind. *How do we get that big bucket up to the roof? Ron surely will not be able to handle it and, to be honest, I am a little bit afraid of heights.* The thought of climbing up that huge long ladder on one hand and holding that big, heavy bucket with the other turned my lower body into an airport; which feels like airplanes circling your nether regions, just without creating any wind effects. *It doesn't matter*, I thought. *I will make it, somehow.*

As Ron and I put the ladder up, we had some difficulty getting it extended to the full length; but we made it and were happy.

Who is going first?" I asked Ron, who was making sure the ladder was safe and secured.

"I'll go, of course," he said.

I was glad not to be the first one because I still felt like I had airplane traffic circling around in my gut! Ron slowly started climbing the ladder, step by step, and after one minute, he almost made it halfway up.

"Are you alright, Ron," I asked?

"Yes, I am just taking a break because I am having some difficulty with my right leg."

Now, he really had my attention. I needed to watch him closer to see how he was doing on the ladder. He resumed climbing and I started laughing when I saw him dancing up the ladder like he was a 1980s break-dancer taking a Zumba class. Long story short, he made it up the ladder and I was glad. My next thought was, *How in the world is he coming back down?* I took the 10 gallon bucket of paint and climbed up to the top of the world, the Patriot Inn.

The roof, of course, is not a normal flat one that is easy to handle. This one has steep angles and there are almost no parts where you can comfortably sit or rest for a minute. By the time I had made it up to the roof, my dear friend Ron had already claimed the one good sitting spot, next to the chimney. Both Ron and the chimney looked like they belonged together. He leaned on the chimney, almost hugging it to absorb the safety and the heat and I was glad he had found a safe place to sit.

"Come on over, Andy. I can hold the bucket so you can roll the paint out and the bucket will be safe with me."

Can he read my mind? I had been wondering where to put the bucket without it spilling over, since the roof was so steep and angled. I was glad Ron had made the offer and I brought him the 10 gallon bucket. I had started covering the first few square feet with the fresh, heavy aluminum paint when I realized Ron was getting nervous.

"Are you alright, Ron?"

"Sure, don't worry. I just have a little cramp in my leg," he replied.

The paint really looked good on the roof. It was shiny, with a reflective silver effect and a smooth consistency. *Almost like a mirror*, I thought, as I turned around to get more paint out from the bucket secured by Ron. His once,seemingly safe seated position now looked very unstable and

I became worried. "Are you alright; or do you need me to stop?" I asked.

"No worries. I've got this," he answered. "I'm just trying to get a very good grip on the bucket and a stable sitting position."

I dumped my roller in the bucket, lifted up the pool of paint and turned 180 degree and proceeded with painting. After rolling the paint out three or four times, I turned around again to refresh my paint roller. As I was turning, I saw Ron sitting with one butt cheek on the roof, two legs in the air, and his hands trying to steady himself. *He made it, good Lord, he made it,* I breathed with a sigh of relief. As that thought was going through my mind, a second thought was slowly forming in my brain....*Where is the bucket?!?!?* As I completed my 180 degree turn, my brain instantly froze. For a moment, I thought maybe there was a hidden camera installed somewhere to film my reaction, just so they could make fun of me. But then I had to face the full impact of Ron's actions. The remaining 9.8 gallons of paint had spilled onto the roof and was working its way down towards the gutters. It looked like a big wave swirling backwards onto the beach. Ron began to stutter and his blood pressure must have gotten a double twin turbo boost because his face turned red like tomato.

"The paint, the paint!" he called, try to save the paint. For a second I thought he had lost his mind because there was no way I could be fast enough to run from the roof down to the sidewalk to catch the paint with the empty bucket. "You need to roll the paint! Hurry up!!"

*Too late,*I thought as I saw the very impressive wave of paint slamming into the gutter. The next thing I remember was the slight calmness I felt when I saw the gutter and instantly calculated nothing will happen because the gutter will catch the paint. Well, that was a total mathematical error, I quickly found out.

Ron's eyes were approximately one inch out of his head as he watched the paint hitting the gutter. And then, there it was, the moment we both will remember for the rest of our lives. The paint hit the gutter as we looked each other in the eyes and thought *Lord, please do not let it go down!* Well, the good Lord must have been on a lunch break at that moment because the paint slammed into the gutter, creating a much higher wave than what was already on the roof, and then it suddenly disappeared. What a lesson in gravity!

Ron eased himself up from his chimney seat and asked me, out of the blue, "How bad is it?"

"Uhhh, I don't know, Ron. I can make it to the edge of the roof and look down, if you want me to."

"Please, look!" he yelled.

I went slowly to the edge because I still had to deal with the remaining paint on the roof and I looked down.

"How bad, how bad is it?" Ron asked.

The only words out of my mouth were, "You don't want to know!!"

It was at that moment that I believe the Lord came back from his lunch break because Ron turned into a 20 years old marathon athlete in zero point zero seconds flat!

I have never before seen a 70+ year old man run quicker down a ladder than him. Before I could even check out the full damage from the roof, I saw Ron walking on the sidewalk, looking for innocent people who may have gotten our self created aluminum rain all over them. Let's put it this way, nobody got hit or injured and the only victims were the historic brick sidewalk and the house.

I climbed down the ladder and walked over to Ron, who was speechless and pale, to get a closer look at what we had caused. We started calculating the damage. First, the siding of the freshly painted white house had to be redone. Second, the bricks on the sidewalk needed to be turned upside down. Third, the aluminum paint would have to be cleaned off the windows. Fourth, the gutter was somehow still holding approximately one gallon of paint, which would have to be cleaned up. Finally, the biggest job was going to be how to tell Verle?

Well, everybody knows how women are and how they always have a sense or a feeling about things. We weren't four minutes into our man's discussion when guess who showed up to check on our roof painting progress?

I will never forget Verle's expression. It was both outrageous and funny all at the same time. Ron started hyperventilating again and cut her off right away.

"We will fix this and don't ever, ever ask me how it all happened!!!" he roared.

Our day ended with rum and Cokes around the kitchen island and all three of us talking about the funny story. We had tears in our eyes from laughing so hard. I walked home that night, looking like an aluminum snow man and smiling the entire way, as I reflected upon our adventure on that cold spring day in May.

18

THE UNCHAINED MELODY
By Ella Verle Weiss

Sophia was a Christian Iranian raised in California. She and her family were flying to London. She was thirteen and her brother nine. The family arrived at the LAX Airport only to discover that the children's passports had expired. They were all in panic mode! Her father had to contact a familiar travel agency so they could fly the next day. They arrived at the *check in* at the very same time they had the previous day.

A young man, Thomas, with his family arrived at the same airport, same day, and also boarded the same plane. Tom's background was different from Sophie's. He spent his childhood in Massachusetts.

Shortly after getting seated on the plane, Sophie and Tom began conversing. Though they began as strangers to each other, they formed a bond of friendship and exchanged addresses in London.They conversed for three years. Then all correspondence stopped.

Four years after they had lost contact, Tom contacted Sophie. They happily reunited and married in Smithfield,

Virginia at the historical St. Paul's Episcopal Church. The two lovers told and celebrated their story at their wedding rehersal dinner on the beautiful sailing ship called the Rover.

Just hours before the marriage ceremony, Sophie and her family left Portsmouth, got lost, and arrived at the church a half hour late.

Her grandparents, uncles and aunts ended up in Yorktown. They took the wrong highway due to wrong directions on the map that was given to them.

Meanwhile, Tom's aunt was entertaining the guests in the church reading a brochure of the old church while walking up and down the aisles.

Sophie was ready to walk down the aisle, when the rest of her family walked in the church door! The marriage ceremony was beautiful and continued without interruption!

"Oh, my love my darling, I've hungered for your touch, a long lonely time."

19

MISTAKEN IDENTITY
By Ronald D. Weiss

One day I was very stressed. *Skinny* Lloyd Saunders and my wife Verle, sent me to Kentucky Fried Chicken to buy some chicken dinners. It just so happened that Kentucky Fried Chicken and McDonald's were very close to each other.

In my stressed state, I mistakenly stopped at McDonald's drive thru to order chicken. The attendant asked what I would like.

I answered into the speaker, "I'd like 3-2 piece white meat chicken dinners with cole slaw and green beans."

"I am sorry, sir. We do not have that!"

"Well, do you have chicken tenders?" I asked.

"No, sir, we do not have that either!"

"Well, give me whatever you have in chicken!" I retorted.

I arrived at home ranting and raving about how Kentucky Fried Chicken had such a poor selection.

I offered *Skinny* and Verle the chicken nuggets. Verle's comment was "How come the chicken came in a McDonald's sack?"

The sack told the story!

20

FRACTURED BEDS
By Ella Verle Weiss

Ruth and Richard were inn-sitters while we vacationed in Europe for three weeks.

A lady guest was a very unhappy person who complained about everything. She arrived three days early to await her partner. She came down for coffee one morning after he had arrived. She told Ruth the bed had broken down.

Ruth rushed up and peeked into the bedchamber thinking the guest was up and dressed. However, he was still in the broken bed. His body laid in a v shape where the broken board had caused the mattress to buckle. She backed out and apologized as she did not expect him to be in bed.

Ruth had moved the woman to another room earlier. The couple ate breakfast and left without leaving a mailing address or paying.

Richard measured the board, and had a new one made. The fixed bed was ready for the next couple.

An innkeeper has to prepare for guests like this, and be congenial. Most guests are not like this. We had only five very unpleasant guests in twelve plus years.

21

BEYOND THE CALL OF DUTY:
By Ella Verle Weiss

One night when all of our guests were in bed, Ron and I were reading in the library. The doorbell rang. It was ten o'clock. We went to the door and to our surprise we saw a taxi cab parked outside.

The cab driver asked, in a Spanish dialect "Do you have a room to rent, and if so, how much will it cost?"

I told him, "We have one room. It will cost one hundred and twenty dollars plus tax."

He hesitated, looked at us, and related this story. The young girl in his cab did not have much money. He had picked her up at the airport, because she did not know how to get to Portsmouth, nor where she would stay. She had paid an organization three thousand dollars to come to the States, and work in our local restaurant. The restaurant was helping sponsor her.

I was very familiar with the fear associated with being in a foreign country. Our family hosted two foreign exchange sons, one from Ecuador and the other from Germany. I was the American Field Service Club sponsor when I taught at the High School in Denison, Iowa.

I could not even imagine being in a strange place without contacts and at night! Ron and I looked at each other, and immediately said. "Forty dollars will do."

The next morning we told Alejandra that she could stay for two weeks free. We would help her find someplace to stay. She was a beautiful gracious girl, and we felt we needed to protect her.

She went to her job every evening. During the days, she looked for an apartment with the other new arrivals from other countries. They worked in the same business. I went to meet her manager. I told him we were aware of her working conditions. I warned him that if anyone mistreated her, he would be talking to City Management.

The manager was compassionate, and well aware of the situation these young people were in. We both agreed to take good care of them. Alejandra moved in a large apartment located in her friends house. I could check on her occasionally. She stopped to see us often, bringing her many friends along.

Her boyfriend came and stayed with her for a month. They went to New York City for a week before they returned to Argentina. When they arrived here from their New York trip, we took them out to dinner. Then they were on their way back home and into the arms of their awaiting families.

Alejandra has emailed me at Christmas many times. I can still see her beautiful face as she stood on the steps of the Inn that spring night!

22

HOUSE UNDER ATTACK
By Ronald D.Weiss

We hosted a wedding shower at the Inn for our granddaughter, Nicole Petersen and her fiance' William Smith.

A total of five baby opossum entered the house too. Someone had left the basement door open The first we knew about them was when we saw our peaches in the kitchen basket. Something or someone had disturbed them. They had small bites in them.We called Dana to ask Ashley if her son Noah had done this. She said, "No, he doesn't like peaches."

Soon after, Michael Kascielniak told our daughter-in-law Tracy that some young opossum was running behind her.

She laughed, "That's not true!" Then she discovered it was behind her, and jumped.

Our grandson Grant followed the opossum into the bathroom. He coaxed it into a cage. Our son David took photos of the opossum in the trap.

Then we discovered there was not just one, but five opossums. We captured them and I took them to a park about eight blocks away. That wasn't the end of the story.

Robert Lemasters told us later that three of them had walked into Clare Vara's garage. She lived near the park. I took one of them to a larger park in Port Norfolk. It never returned.

23

A PLACE IN OUR HEARTS
By Ella Verle Weiss

[Note: *Ron and I have always had a special place in our hearts for young people, because we were always teachers or professors. Our lives continuously spun around them including our own three children.*]

It was a late afternoon of one fall October day when the door bell rang. I opened the door, and there stood a handsome young sailor dressed in his casuals. He was about 19 years old.

He stepped in with a big smile and asked, "Do you have a room for two nights?"

"Yes," I replied.

Shortly after, we ushered him into the Lafayette bedchamber. He ordered pizza from a local pizza place and took it to his room. He settled in for the night.

The next morning the young man came down for breakfast. He enthusiastically ate every bit of our usual large English breakfast.

We visited with him, for we were interested in his background.

"I'm from Texas," he said. He described his family and talked about home briefly. He wanted to spend the days with Ron and me. We discovered he was very homesick. We paid as much attention as we could while attending to our other guests.

When he was ready to leave he gave us a check. We found out later that we could not cash it. His account lacked the necessary funds.

A week later a credit agency called us and asked if we would file a complaint against him as he was AWOL (absent without leave). He had left other places with bad checks. We said we could not help. He had already left and left no mailing address.

The agent got angry with us and said, "You are just encouraging such bad behavior."

We told the man on the phone, "We will not file a complaint. He is young and homesick. Give him a break."

24

INDECENT EXPOSURE
By Ronald D. Weiss

One evening we had the Lafayette room booked for a honeymoon couple. The Lee bedchamber next to it we had booked to a financial consultant. We expected the couple later that night.

Our suite was located on the top floor. We had to pass both of these bedchamber doors on our way upstairs. Verle went to bed early that evening. Both bedchamber doors were still open. She noticed that the man in the Lee bedchamber was talking on the phone in the nude. Fortunately, he didn't notice her. She stepped back into the Lafayette bedchamber. When I came upstairs Verle stood in the darkened room and pointed to the Lee room. Then I joined her, and we both went on up to our suite.

We worried about the honeymoon couple arriving and seeing the nude man. Would they wonder what kind of inn we were running?

The next morning the Lafayette door was still open and no one had been there. Fortunately the young honeymoon couple had stayed overnight at the place where they married. The person from the Lee room had checked out. The married couple stayed with us the next night.

DECENT EXPOSURE.
By Ronald D. Weiss

One cold winter night, a frequent guest Steve Carl was sleeping in the Lee Room. That bedchamber normally had a pleasant temperature.

That evening, however, it continued getting hotter and hotter. Steve slept in his boxer shorts and opened the door wide open. He was hot!

The next morning we discovered the basement outside door standing open. It had been open all night causing the hot air to enter mainly the Lee Room.

It was almost a repeat of the nude man's story. However, this time the door had to be open to cool the room. Also, Steve dressed decently.

Steve stayed frequently with us. He and his wife Kay eventually moved to Portsmouth. We remain dear friends.

THE SUPERBOWL PARTY
By Ronald D. Weiss

The night of a Super Bowl, we decided to have a Super Bowl party for friends and workers of Mike Koscielniak. About 25 people attended. The parlor was the best place to watch TV. We have a small knot hole in our heart of pine floor. We ran the cord to our largest TV through it. We had an enjoyable evening watching on the Inns' largest TV.

LET IT GO!
By Ella Verle Weiss

Grocery shopping can be a stressful experience when you own an Inn. You are always in a hurry!

We were in Norfolk on this particular shopping trip.I wanted to go to Harris Teeter, as they had the unusual items I always needed. Ron stayed in the van with his newspaper, while I ran into the store.

I hurriedly picked up 26 items instead of the number needed for the Express lane. I was not paying attention and pushed my cart into an express lane where the clerk immediately started scanning my purchases. A young man and his girl companion behind me complained loudly. The girl openly expressed her feelings as the young man continued his harassment.

I asked the clerk to let me go to another check out. She immediately reacted to the young man's rude behavior. He was not going to get his way. That was for certain.

"No," The clerk declared emphatically, "He can wait!"

They opened another express lane so we checked out at the same time. We passed. I told the rude young man that he badly needed an attitude adjustment!

He chased me out of the store. He continued yelling at me. "Go... yourself." He yelled at me 15 times.

I pointed a finger at him telling him that he needed *to grow up!*

His girlfriend finally convinced him to *let it go*. I was close to the van by this time only to find my husband asleep and the door locked. Ron quickly opened the door when I knocked on the window.

I settled into my seat, looked to see the young man speed rapidly past in his SUV. I wondered what planet he lived on!

I had tried to correct the situation to no avail. I had never experienced any situation like this in any of my earlier 33 years of teaching.

I hooked my seat belt, took a deep breath, and said to myself, "Let it go!"

28

STOLEN BOOKS
By Ronald D. Weiss

Verle and I were watching television late one night and there was a knock on the door.

We looked out to see two older men standing by the door. Unfortunately, we decided to let them in because they said that the last place they stopped would not let them stay. They had dogs in their car. The other hotel would let them keep both dogs, if the two men shampooed them. The two men got mad and left that hotel.

We agreed to help them for the evening. The one younger man went to bed, the older one said he would stay up for awhile. The next morning we noticed our library bookshelf had all been rearranged, He scattered books throughout our library and parlour. When we finally got them on their way, we noticed some of our older books were missing.

They wanted to stay another evening or two with us. I told the older man. "We run *a high class place*, and can not allow you to stay another night."

The older man became belligerent and said "So you don't think we are good enough for you?"

I felt threatened by him and called my son Denton. He and our friend Andy came over.

The next day I read in The Virginia Pilot Newspaper that the police had arrested the older man. He was the same man. He had gone back to the same hotel, they had tried to stay at the previous night. The men hadn't washed their dogs. They put the older man in jail with a $3000 bail for animal negligence.

We didn't try to reclaim any books, because we just wanted him to get out of jail and leave town.

29

THE SCREENWRITER
By Ella Verle Weiss

It was later in the evening approximately 8:00 pm, and all the guests were checked in when I answered the phone. The voice on the other line asked, "Is this the Patriot Inn? Do you have labels on the door of your common room?"

At his point I stopped him. " Wait!" and said, "Who are you? Why are you asking me these questions?"

He gave me his name and said, "I am a screenwriter in Los Angeles, California."

"But Wait." I said, "Why the questions?"

He began relating his story. Everyone visiting the Inn had a story.

He continued," I was dreaming and I dreamed I was at the Patriot Inn." Then he paused a moment.

"Is there a social room to the right when you come into the entry hall?"

I answered ,"Yes."

He continued on with the description of the room, the arrangement of the sofa, chairs, and tables. He described the people visiting there in little groups at times and other times in larger groups.

"Well," he said , "I was sitting on the sofa when the man sitting on a chair across from me stood up, and said, while handing me a ten dollar bill, 'Give me the names of the ten people.' In the dream I stood up instantly and said 'Wait, I am alive,' and his reply was, 'Yes, and I am dead.'"

We continued our conversation and he asked me "Do you know what he meant by the ten?"

The screenwriter said he had awakened,tried to go back to sleep, and finish his dream, but he could not. He went to his computer and tried to locate the Patriot Inn which he did. Thus the telephone call to figure out the answer.

I said I would try to understand, but asked him where he was from originally. I had noted he had a distinct dialect. He was from Massachusetts, and spent much time on the East Coast. I then suggested on his next trip, he should visit the Inn here in Virginia.

His last comment was, " I have already been there, but if you find out about the ten people call me."

Two years later at 8:00 am. Eastern Time I called him. When he answered he retorted, "Lady, do you know what time it is here?"

It was 4:00 am. in California. I told him we were

going to be on HGTV Restore America the following week and we still had not found out what the ten meant.

He responded ," Okay! Goodbye."

A few weeks later we met the Williams family members, who had lived here in the 1970's . They came for a visit and wanted to tell us the history of the Inn. They shared all that they knew about our house, prior to our occupancy. They knew of a man named Paul Grote who stayed here when it was a rooming house. He had passed away in the parlour. The same room that the screenwriter had talked to the *"dead man standing."*

THE GOVERNMENT DIGNITARY
By Ronald D. Weiss

One late afternoon our guests were having their wine, cheese, and crackers in the parlor. We had another guest arrive at the door. A well dressed man and a big marine dressed in his fatigues stood with him at the doorway. I took the well dressed man upstairs to his room. The Marine with him stayed behind and spoke to Verle. "Be sure you lock the door when I leave."

Verle thought that was strange. She assumed he must think that the Inn was not a safe area. She spoke her thoughts out loud to our other guests. Immediately the marine stepped back into the hall and said abruptly, "I said to lock the door."

We found out later that the well dressed guest held a high office in the government. He had spoken at Langley air base that day. He was going to speak to the Joint Forces Command the next day.

THE FLANNEL NIGHTGOWN
By Ella Verle Weiss

There was a beautiful young woman in her thirties who was staying with us from the Los Angeles area. She had owned a bridal shop in Chino, California. She and her husband a part time actor owned a home. They had purchased a cottage in the hills just above LA, not too far away.

She had ordered wedding gowns for many young women in the surrounding areas from France. Unfortunately, the company sent all the gowns at once rather then on the planned basis, as the weddings occurred. The total cost for the gowns was excessively high. It far exceeded her resources. The bank closed the doors to her business. She inherited screaming young women and their enraged fiances.

We were talking in the library as the story unfolded. I could see this was not going to be a pretty scene. She continued her story. One night her husband, his friend and she were at their cottage in the hills. If you have ever been in the mountains at night, you know it is pitch black with the forestation. She decided after dinner to go for a walk by herself. She left the men to their manly conversations.

She stood at the porch and slowly lit a cigarette to calm her nerves. She knew the week was not going to be good. She would have to console distressed *brides to be*. She had to walk and think how she could resolve this problem.

About half a mile from the cabin two young men grabbed her. They beat her and covered her with limbs and leaves, leaving her for dead.

While looking at his watch and seeing how late it was her husband became concerned. So he and his friend started looking for her. They finally found her alive, but she was in poor condition. They put her in their SUV and went to the closest hospital.

The next morning her husband had to fly to New York for a photo shoot. He put her on an airplane for Norfolk, Virginia where her father and mother lived. She was in the hospital for a week, then her father scheduled her to stay at the Inn. Her parents did not have extra room, as they were renovating an old house and had no space.

The first few days went fine as she unraveled this whole story to me again. I have always been a good listener.

I heard an ambulance on the street in the middle of her third night here. I asked Ron where they were stopping. A loud knock sounded on our bedroom door. We were in bed and I was wearing my long sleeved flannel nightgown. I stood shocked in front of the EMT.

Our guest had an anxiety attack and called 911. He said,"You need to come now. She wants you!" I rushed down the stairs in a panic mode to the ambulance. They pushed me into the vehicle to calm her down. They said she wanted me to go with her. I insisted she needed immediate help. I promised her that I would call her parents. They lived across the street.

I could not go to the hospital in a flannel nightgown. Running around dressed like this in public embarrassed me. After talking to her for a half hour, she agreed she would be okay until her parents arrived.

She did not come back after she left the hospital as she stayed with her parents for awhile. One day on the street I asked her father how she was. He responded that she was slowly recovering.

About six months later a woman guest with her husband had a slight heart attack in the night. They called 911. The EMTS drove the ambulance to the Inn. I watched again wearing my favorite flannel nightgown. I wondered if the stairwell was going to hold the gurney holding his wife, and the two heavy EMTS. I need not have concerned myself. Everything went okay.

The next day after the event passed, her husband told me something. When he had called 911 they said. "Oh, we know where that is, the owner wears a flannel nightgown."

I often wonder if they knew I owned four flannel nightgowns, all in different colors.

"Their aunt married a young navy man

stationed in Portsmouth."

HIGH POINT LANDING

Photograph is by Alison S. Elder

32

AMONG HER SOUVENIRS
By Ella Verle Weiss

Summers are always hot and humid in Virginia, but the breezes across the water makes it very pleasant. It was a hot balmy day when Margaret from New York and her sister Jennifer from Connecticut arrived. It was late afternoon around 5:00 pm. We usually served wine, cheese, and crackers at that time.

They brought a mystery along with their luggage. The mystery they shared with us. They were on a demanding mission. Their Aunt had passed away. Their aunt's will stated she wanted her large estate divided among her four children, three girls and one boy. However, none of the family had ever heard of the boy or girl.

The two sisters gave their cousins, Margaret and Jennifer a promise. If Margaret and Jennifer could find the two missing children, the two sisters would gladly share the estate. The two missing children would be in their seventies.

The two cousins spent many hours at the library and mortuaries while staying at the Inn. They found neither the Boy nor the girl listed as dead. Through many days of

99

searching they made a discovery. Their aunt married a young navy man stationed in Portsmouth at the time of the second world war. They had two children. The boy and girl Margaret and Jennifer were trying to find.

Portsmouth increased from a population of six thousand to forty thousand during World War II. The government needed workers. The factory and shipyards brought thousands of people from all over the United States to Portsmouth. Their Aunt was one of those who worked at the sewing factory. She made uniforms and other items for the military stationed overseas. This earlier population surge made Margaret and Jennifer's job difficult. They found their aunt's married name, and then discovered her young navy husband had died in the war.

When her husband died, she had little money from her job. Therefore, she left the two children with a street vender. The vender sold food to the textile workers during the day.

She eventually met another young officer. She was nineteen at the time. The children became a burden, as there were many officer parties, dancing, and other activities at the USO. She gave the children to the woman vender, and moved on with this new life. She married and moved to New York City with her husband when the war was over.

The vender continued to care for the children. A few years later, the factory closed, and she could no longer care for both children. She gave the little boy to a friend who could raise him.

Margaret and Jennifer had stayed long enough at the Inn to find another contact. Someone knew of the vender who had died. After receiving that information, they returned home. They once again gathered with their New York cousins to discuss their findings. This time they sorted through every paper and memorabilia their Aunt had left in her extensive library. Stunningly, among her souvenirs they found a love letter written to her when she was sixteen. It was from a young man who wanted to run away to the South and join the Navy.

In the fall of that same year, Margaret again returned to Portsmouth. This time she came by herself. She stayed with the people who had information about the children. When I visited with her for the last time, they had some clues to their whereabouts. Nothing was definite.

We never saw Margaret again. However, she sent two butterfly tea pot clips that would catch tea drips from the teapot spout. Attached to the gift was a note that stated they had found the cousins. They were going to inherit their share of the large estate. The family was anxious to welcome, and embrace their new family members.

When I use the drip catchers and look at the two butterflies, I think of the two beautiful children, and the passion that Margaret and Jennifer displayed! They were going to catch these two butterflies and never let them go. Why do some families have a passion to reunite, while others take family relationships so casually.

"After their stay in New York City,

they would ride a bus to

Norfolk, Virginia."

33

THE NEW YORK BUS
By Ella Verle Weiss

Joelle Le Pelletier whose mother was the daughter of Ernest Weiss in Colmar France called from Strasbourg, France. These are all cousins of Ron, the old Weiss family in France. She called us and told us she was coming to stay for a week and bringing two friends. One friend was a young woman Simone. The other friend was Alain, a young man.

Joelle got so excited about the trip. After their stay in New York City, they would ride a bus to Norfolk, Virginia. She declared how inexpensive the bus ride was. We would pick them up at the bus stop.

I thought it was horrifying, when I heard of their choice of transportation! I put the phone down and rushed to tell Ron. We had heard about these cheap bus lines. Just two months before, one of their buses had gone off the road in the middle of the night. Seventeen passengers died.

We decided to call her back and try to persuade her to choose some other transportation to Virginia. Unfortunately she had already paid for the ticket with no chance of a refund. These bus drivers speak no English let alone French.

They drive nearly 24 hours with no sleep. They dump their passengers off, then pick up those people who have return tickets to New York City.

If I could not change the plans of our relatives. I would meet Joelle, Simone, and Alain at a specified parking lot in Norfolk, and transport them to the Inn.

It happened they would be arriving at 11:30 pm. Ron had to fly back to Charter Oak, Iowa, for one of his alumni reunions. I had to be the one to pick them up at Norfolk.

The evening arrived. Much to my surprise our friends Dottie and Irvin Lindley stopped in for a late night cocktail. I was like an attack dog, as I ushered them in and served each of us a rum in coke.

Next, I told them of my problem of having to pick Joelle up at the bus stop. I did not even know its exact location. Dottie said that she and one of her friends had ridden this bus line before. She and Irv agreed to go with me. Irv drove the van and Dottie was the navigator.

We arrived at the parking lot where the bus stopped for the passengers. We waited about one hour and a white bus drove up with no sign or identification. Dottie and I got out of the van, thinking our family would be getting off. After looking through the group, we discovered they were not there.

Dottie pushed me on to the bus. She said, " Ask if there were any Caucasians on this bus?" A handsome young African American man told me he thought they had gotten off at the Virginia Beach Stop.

The time was getting into the early morning, and Irv was now driving. Dottie was complaining about his fast driving. I was frantic not knowing where these people were. This is an unusual area of the U.S. with all its' water ways.

We pulled up to the Virginia Beach Stop noticing a group of people gathered outside. The bus just pulled away as we pulled in. I ran into the restaurant. They said they had seen three people pulling suitcases toward a hotel on the beach. I rejoined my friends in our vehicle.

We drove over the brush on a sandy road to the hotel. We found it closed. It was 2:00 am. I desperately called our son from my cell phone. He responded. "Mom do you realize what time it is? Let them get a taxi. You get home. I have surgery tomorrow."

With that conversation, we headed home only to discover the three sitting on the front porch with their luggage. They figured we were looking for them. They hired a taxi and drove to look for us. They decided to go to the Inn and wait.

"She met him at the door

in a little black dress

and black heels."

34

THE LITTLE BLACK DRESS
By Ronald D. Weiss

Some interesting experiences happened to Mike Koscielniak who stayed here often. He supervised at the Joint Forces Command. He worked for Los Alamos Labs in New Mexico as well. The Portsmouth-Norfolk area was one of his assignments.

Many times he brought other assistants with him to the Inn. He became friends with many of our friends and customers. We often did various activities with him. He also became friends of our son Dr. Denton Weiss, his wife Michelle, and their two daughters.

Our 19 year old granddaughter Ashley Petersen worked at the Inn one summer for us. So Mike jokingly spoke to her. "The next time I come down I will take you out to dinner."

He was like an uncle to our granddaughters. Mike called ahead of time when he was in town. He suggested that we all go out for dinner.

When he arrived Ashley met him at the door in a little black dress and black heels and jokingly said, "So, where are we going?" You can imagine Mike's surprise! We all laughed as we went out for dinner together.

35

DIDN'T WE HAVE FUN?
By Ella Verle Weiss

This is a sad event that we experienced. We have made friends of many of our guests. Jill Mumie worked at Kodak in Ghent, Norfolk, Virginia. She wanted her parents to visit the Tidewater-Portsmouth area. Her parents lived in Pitman, New Jersey. She came to look at the Patriot in preparation for their visit. Ron and I loved her energy and beautiful personality so it was a *fit*. They would stay with us.

We became instant friends of Jill's parents, Walt and Betty Jean, BJ as we called her. They came many times through the years, and one year Walt even purchased one of my paintings for BJ. Betty Jean and I talked often on the telephone. Our conversations included our NSDAR projects, their son, Jefferey (Kathy) and grandchildren. Jill's activities were also in our personal news.

She called us in 2011 to tell us that the doctors had diagnosed Walt with terminal cancer. She called us after his death on October 9, 2012. She explained that on his death bed she had asked him, "Would you do it again?" She meant, "Would you marry me again?"

His response was "Didn't we have fun!"

BJ and I cried. Recalling this story causes me to cry while I write. *Love without end, Amen.*

36

BUSTLING
By Ella Verle Weiss

Our granddaughter Ashley flew in from Houston for her photo shoot in her wedding dress at the Chrysler museum in Norfolk. After the shoot, I asked her to come over so we could get pictures of her on our beautiful Colonial staircase.

She arrived shortly before our guests. I decided to have Ulla and I bustle Ashley's long wedding train for a different pose.

Now I had not told Ulla before what *bustling* was. It is pulling the train of the bride's dress up and buttoning it usually near the waist on the underside of the dress. This creates a beautiful fullness and the bride can then dance.

Ulla and I were under the train trying to find the buttons when the door bell rang. Two business men arrived at the door. Ulla was still holding much of the train which I had dropped to open the door. It was a peculiar scene for the men and they asked what we were doing? To which I responded "Bustling."

Ashley was facing them so they could not see her

derriere. They commented that they would gladly help. We assured them we were adequate for the task at hand. We found the buttons, secured the train. Ashley got another breathtaking photo of her in her wedding.

Ulla Geduldig Yatrofsky

"I had not told Ulla before,

what bustling was."

Ashley Petersen Kerr On Our Grand Staircase

Ashley In Bustled Wedding Dress

37

LIMITED ACCESS
By Ella Verle Weiss

One warm spring day we had a young woman fashion magazine editor from New York call for a reservation. We agreed that she would check in with her husband at 7:00 pm and stay in the Lee chamber. The couple still had not arrived at 1:00 am. We assumed they were not coming. We trudged up the steps to our third floor suite.

The next morning Ron and I woke up tired. I showered in our suite. The other bath-showers were all in use. I assured Ron that this couple was not coming. I assured him that he should hop in the shower of the Lee chamber for a quick scrub.

It shocked me when the doorbell rang, and this couple showed up at the door. I knew my amazement was showing on my face. I asked them why they were so late. They told me their story. I had an immediate visual mind flash of Ron in their shower.

What was I going to do? They wanted to use the toilet immediately, and then go directly to bed. They had been fighting all the way here, and then had continued driving around Portsmouth the rest of the night. First she didn't want to come here to the Inn because they were so late for their reservation.

I told them that Ron was in their shower, because of our predicament with shower use. We had five bathrooms

but four of them were in use! They went into their bedchamber after I rushed in and closed the bathroom door between the rooms. Ron had to jump out of the shower to unlock the door to the hall, so I could get in.

They had to attend a wedding by 2:00 pm so they had about four hours of sleep.

They stayed the whole weekend and turned out to be a wonderful couple. She gave us magazines from her company which we shared with our granddaughters.

Innkeepers do not get a lot of sleep!

38

THE PARKERS
By Ella Verle Weiss

The Patriot Inn's name endeared us to many military personnel. We had many guests from the different branches. The following is one of their stories. It began with the Parkers, an engaged couple.

The Parkers booked the Patriot for their wedding night and weekend. They also booked rooms for their wedding party. All the guests were young helicopter pilots out of Langley Airforce Base, both men and women.

Ron and I loved the lively energy of young people. That is one reason we liked being professors. They made us feel young and happy. This was a group of adventurous young people.

I was on my own at the inn, as Ron had a prior commitment. He had a class reunion with his former basketball coach and team at Charter Oak, Iowa.

The couples arrived and checked into their bedchambers. They prepared themselves for the next big day which was their wedding day.

I was preparing the tables and appointments for the next mornings breakfast. I wanted everything to go smoothly. The Parkers had a wonderful wedding day. The evening after the wedding, the small party all came back. The young men other than the bridegroom gathered on the veranda for beers, cocktails, and cigars. I was looking after them as usual.

I loved the busy activities of the young women preparing themselves for bed. The young men were laughing and you could feel the aura of all their masculinity.

Now I am a romantic. I was taking wine glasses and plates from the parlour to the kitchen and overheard an intimate conversation. The best man's wife peeked out the door to the veranda. She told him she was running her bath water. After that statement she elegantly ascended the stairs.

I opened the door wide enough to speak to her husband. I whispered to him. "I know when a beautiful young woman tells her lover that she was preparing a bath, he has an obligation in life to take advantage of it."

As I closed the door I heard him say to the others "She is one classy lady, isn't she?"

He joined his wife in their bedchamber shortly after.

I picked up my baskets of towels and walked to our third floor suite. I was happy that I had lived such an exciting life and could exchange thoughts and ideas with these young beautiful patriots

The Parker couple returned to the Patriot for their anniversary. This time with only one of the young men along to celebrate. That was the last time we saw them.

I can only imagine these pilots flying their copters. I believe they keep us safe both here and across the world. I have this wonderful feeling that upon occasion they are in the sky looking down on us. I am sure they remember their wedding party too.

Sometimes when we are out on the veranda eating, we hear a copter flying overhead. I always wave my hand, thinking if might be one of the wonderful couples who had gathered here.

"After we completed our work,

I felt like entering the church, and

praying 'Thank you!'"

39

FIRE ON HIGH STREET
By Ronald D. Weiss

Skip-jack Nautical Wares is one of the finest maritime shops on the east coast. It offers an extensive selection of nautical antiques, marine art, furniture, and decor. Joseph and Alison S. Elder own Skip-jack. It was and is a popular local tourist shop. It is a nautical art gallery mixed with ship artifacts of all kinds.

Our son David M. Weiss a professional artist had an open house to sell his art in the former Skip-jack gallery. The night after the open house sale, the tourist shop had a devastating fire. The city did not allow anyone into the building before they pushed the building down.

We had no idea of the condition of David's paintings. The next morning I went down to see if any his paintings were undamaged. A police officer was there. He said, "You can go on in. I believe if you work fast, you can pull out most of his paintings."

Fortunately, my son, Denton and his wife Michelle were with me. We got excited when we discovered David's paintings had minimum damage. My son and his wife took the paintings down to their vehicle, parked near the Catholic Church. After we completed our work, I felt like entering the church and praying "Thank you!" It was definitely a spiritual moment.

40

OOPS!
By Ella Verle Weiss

Ron, Ulla, and I were pulling ivy off the side of the house when I decided to use Ulla's long handled clippers. "Oops!" I had just clipped through a wire connecting the thermostat to the air conditioner. It quit running!

I looked to see if Ron noticed. Ulla told me excitedly, "Here he comes!" He suddenly quit working and walked toward me. He swore about the mess that I had accidentally created.

I had to get someone to fix it immediately. So I got quotes for the repair. Clem's bid was the low bid. I was happy about that, because I knew he was a good electrician.

We had guests coming in and it was one of the hottest days in September!

"I could neither hear her answer,

nor could I see her facial expression;

but I am convinced, knowing her long enough,

she rolled her pretty eyes and fell back onto her bed,

mumbling to Ron,

"Oh my gosh. That is really early!"

41

ROAD RUNNER VERSUS THE TRASH MAN
By Andi Bongiovi

Unedited and unabridged.

The phone rang at around 8:00 am on a Thursday morning, just as I was stepping out of the house to walk my Rottweiler, Orca and to fill my lungs with fresh, crisp air before working on the honey do list from my lovely wife, Nannette. I picked up the phone and answered, "Yes?"

"Hey, Andy. It's Ron from the Patriot Inn," he whispered, "and I would like to ask you if you've got time tomorrow to paint one of the rooms before the weekend because we have guests coming tomorrow."

Since I didn't have any other plans for Friday, aside from putting out the trash can, I answered, "Yes. I will be there around 7:00 am, if you don't mind. This way I will have the entire Friday morning and half of the afternoon to fix whatever needs to be done before the first guest arrives." There was silence on the other end of the phone for several seconds and I thought the line had gone dead. "Ron? Can you hear me? Are you still there?"

"Uh, yeah I am. Uh, what time did you say?"

"I will be there at 7:00 am."

Again, there was silence and then I could hear him whispering to Verle, "He will be here around 7:00 am. We have to be up by then!"

I could neither hear her answer, nor could I see her facial expression; but I am convinced, knowing her long enough, she rolled her pretty eyes and fell back onto her bed, mumbling to Ron, "Oh my gosh. That is really early!"

Then Ron came back to me and said, "How about 8:00 am?"

Now, I knew for sure that Verle had fallen back onto her bed and had rolled her eyes like a Ferris wheel! "Ron, don't worry. I have a key and can let myself in. I will be very quiet and will let you sleep."

"OK, that sounds good," he said, "and I will make breakfast when I get up.

Another project at the Patriot Inn, I thought, *which always ends up in laughter, rum and cokes, and some cute little stories.* I was wondering what the next day would bring.

To me, the Patriot Inn always looks like a museum from the inside out. I will never stop admiring the decor in each room! Old colonial style pictures telling stories: from hunting with dogs in the autumn to coach rides with white horses in the spring and ice skating in the winter, all circa 1800. I often catch myself standing in front of a picture and dreaming up a story in my head of how it would be if we still had those times today. The antique furniture with the warm, shiny wooden floors and the old windows and chandeliers make everybody feel like they've gone back 200 years in time. It is so peaceful and quiet, you can hear the grandfather clock from the second floor on almost every level of the house. Ron and Verle always try to give the guests as much comfort and silence as possible. The Patriot Inn was also known as The Sleep Inn.

My Friday started very smooth and lovely because I got up at the same time as my wife and she made us a wonderful breakfast. The sun was up already and we were talking about our plans for the weekend. The coffee tasted just perfect and with the windows opens in the kitchen of our old house, I didn't want to leave. I gave my wife a kiss, wished her a nice day, and took the keys to the Patriot Inn with me. Usually, I walk over there; but I drove on this day because I had to take some tools and my small radio; which gave me company during my projects.

I opened the door very slowly and gently, so as not to make any noise. I closed the door and held my breath for a second to listen for sounds of anyone stirring. Silence. Again, I felt the warm welcome and quiet atmosphere in the entrance hall. The only sound I could hear was from the ticking of the grandfather clock on the second level.

I went down to the basement to get the paint and ladder out, so I could begin painting the first room. On my way back, I thought I should get some old newspapers to protect the floor from any paint spills or splatters. All of the old newspapers are kept in a basket in the kitchen. The hallway leading from the entrance way back to the kitchen has some tricky steps in between the foyer and the dining room and you have to be mobile to climb up or down them. Those steps are very important to me because they give me a pretty clear indication of how Ron and Verle are feeling physically on any given day. If Ron uses the hand rail only for balance and to go up and down the steps at a normal gait, then I know he is feeling good and not having back pain or stiffness. If he takes a break on each step and looks around, as if to be sure nobody can see him pausing, then I know he had a rough night and is in pain. Verle, on the other hand, has fooled me several times because she has a tendency to stop on the first or second step and just start talking to me or asking questions. So trying to gauge her health in the morning is like playing Russian roulette with a good morning story on the hallway steps.

The Patriot Inn has two doors to enter the house. The door to the main entrance is at the front of the house and, of course, is for guests. The second door is in the kitchen at the back of the house and is mostly used for taking out the garbage and for bringing the groceries into the house. Both doors are always kept secure. To access the house you have to use a key or ring the doorbell. Otherwise, you cannot get into the B&B. The kitchen door only has a door knocker on it; which always startles me whenever somebody uses it.

The first room I had to paint was the parlor. It is immediately adjacent to the foyer which, made it much easier for me to bring the ladder and the paint into the house. The kitchen door is all the way at the back of the house and didn't do me any good that morning. But, I checked it anyway to make sure nobody could come in and just in case Ron had forgotten to lock it last night. I discovered it was securely locked.

I went back to the parlor, put up the ladder and used a small paint brush to apply the first coat of paint o those areas where the roller could not reach. Twenty minutes into my project, I heard somebody walking down the stairs from the second level to the main floor.

"Good morning, Andy! How are you?" welcomed Ron. He was greeting me with a smile on his face and I could not tell if he was in pain or not.

"How are you this morning?" I asked.

"Well, I think I am alright," he answered. "I am going to make breakfast. Also, today is trash day and I have hurry up."

"Do you need help with getting the trash can out from behind the house?" I asked.

"No, don't worry. I've got it."

I became suspicious and stepped down from the ladder to do my health check on Ron and watch him go down the hallway steps. *Oh Jesus, Lord have mercy*, I thought. He didn't look too steady on the steps. For a moment, I thought he had become a master of illusion because he literally looked as though he were moving in slow motion. I swear, he was walking so slow, I could probably ties his shoestrings as he was walking!

I started making fun of him and asked, "How is your training exercise coming along? Are you still preparing for the Olympic Games in running the hurdle race?"

He laughed and said, "Yeah, and you are going to nail me some 2X4's flat on the floor, so I can improve my height and flexibility by jumping over those hurdles!"

I started laughing out loud, forgetting Verle was still asleep upstairs. I love joking with Ron because he never fails to shoot back right away and he is able to spice up life. He loves to laugh and he loves to tell stories; which always capture my attention and interest.

I went back to my paint job and after another 15 minutes or so I heard a noise coming from somewhere. It sounded a washing machine on the spin cycle. *It's too early for that*, I thought as I stopped painting. *Where in the world is that noise coming from?* The intensity of the knocking noise increased and I started creating funny pictures in my head.

Could it be a woodpecker on steroids who is trying to knock down the 100 year old oak tree? Or, is it Ron wearing lederhosen and doing his warm up program for the Olympic Games by dancing the Bavarian Schuplattler? I know the dance requires a lot of flexibility; which he would need to jump over those 2X4s anyway! Now, I was really interested in where that noise was coming from and climbed down off of the ladder. As soon as I stepped into the foyer, the noise suddenly stopped. I looked up toward the second level of the house to see if Verle had maybe gotten up and started heading down. Nothing! I started walking back towards the kitchen and noticed Ron was nowhere to be found! I saw the coffee had been prepared; but the breakfast prep area looked like the victim of a Black Friday sales rack: everything was hastily piled upon it with no semblance of order.

Something must have been happen here, I thought as I carefully went to open the kitchen door. It was still locked. Then, I could see somebody walking through the yard. *Lord, please do not let it be a thief or burglar,* I prayed because I had nothing to defend myself with, aside from the 3 inch paint brush in my hand. In the midst of getting nervous and shifting into protection mode, I heard the front door bell ring. The first thing that came to my head was, *what maniac is using the doorbell at this time of the morning when Verle is still taking her beauty sleep?* The doorbell was ringing and ringing. Nonstop, without any breaks at all! *That damned woodpecker,* I thought. *You are done with the oak tree and now you are testing the doorbell!* I started running through the hallway, passing the dining room and jumping all the steps in one leap, thinking if that crazy person doesn't immediately stop torturing the doorbell, I will beat him with the paint brush!

The doorbell kept ringing and I felt my blood pressure going through the roof and my patience getting stretched to the maximum limit when somebody stopped me before I reached the door. It was Verle, in her white nightgown with her hair looking as wild as Pippi Longstocking's and wearing a look that could kill!

"Who is at the door and making all that nerve racking noise out there? I am going to explode!!! Just open the door!!!"

I was still in a little bit of shock and too out of breath to answer her. I opened the door. Verle took a deep breath and was ready to lambast whoever was out there and make sure that person will never ever forget the Patriot Inn policy: first, comfort and second, quiet.

It was Ron, with his hands thrown up in the air and erratically half mumbling and half yelling, "The door is locked and the trash man is here!"

Did the trash man have a gun pulled on him? Why did he have his hands up in the air? I peeked out the door. Nope, nobody else was out there. Only Ron acting like a woman on her menstrual cycle ready to run somebody over! I stepped aside so he could come into the house and receive the full impact of his noisy, painful doorbell misuse. He instantly saw Verle on the stairs waiting to unload on him when he started to scream out, "Don't ask and you had best leave me alone! I have to get to the trash man!"

He started running towards the kitchen and Verle looked at me as if imitating windshield wipers with her hand on her forehead. I didn't know where to look first, or what to answer at all but it really was funny to watch both of them. I instantly had flashbacks to the cartoon of the Road Runner and the coyote. Who is chasing whom? Was Ron the Road Runner and the trash man the coyote?

Verle took the last steps down to the hallway and we both watched Ron disappear. He passed all 4 rooms without pausing or tripping one time: the restroom, the laundry room, the dining room and the kitchen.

"Wow," I said to Verle. "I have never before seen him move that fast in all the years I've known him! I don't know what you fed him for dinner last night; but make sure you give Nannette the recipe! I could have nailed 8X8s on the floor this morning and he still would have made it in no time to the kitchen without any contact or breaks."

Verle finished the breakfast preparations and after setting the table, Ron came in from the outside with a big, satisfied smile on his face.

"Done," he said. "I just paid the garbage man and gave him $20.00!"

My coffee felt like it went down my throat the wrong way and Verle was ready to explode.

"You did what? Are you going to tell me that all of the drama this morning was about $20.00 for the trash man?"

"Yep, you bet!" he said, sitting in his chair and opening the newspaper to settle in for his morning read.

"Well, if a trash collecting day and $20.00 gets you this excited and mobile, then I will change the schedule to every day so we will always have this to laugh about on a daily basis!"

The room painting project was finished just in time for the first guests to arrive that day and this story was shared not only on that evening; but on many other occasions with friends and family.

"My eyes riveted

on a large object on her neck."

***

"Beautiful reflections danced from

the engraved

sterling silver bubbled heart locket."

42

THE SILVER HEART
By Ella Verle Weiss

A beautiful young couple came to the Inn for their anniversary. I invited them in. My eyes riveted on a large object on her neck. The evening sunlight came in through the Inn's windows and shined on her necklace. Beautiful reflections danced from the engraved sterling silver bubbled heart locket. She had hung it on a medium weight sterling silver chain.

The next morning at breakfast, I told her, "I have never seen anything to equal your locket. You must enjoy owning such a piece. It looks so beautiful reflecting the light."

She held the heart up with her hand and responded. "Oh, this is our baby."

I was curious why she considered it her baby. Maybe it was an anniversary gift. However, to my surprise she continued to tell me the story behind it. Their baby had died and they had her body cremated. They put her ashes into this custom designed and engraved heart. She always wore it to be close to her baby. I expressed my condolences and continued to serve breakfast to the couple and our other guests. The other guests tried to subdue their reactions to the young woman's statements.

Two years later, I was selling memorabilia during our community's Ghost Walk Tour. She came to the table where I was working. She surprised me, but I was happy to see her and her husband again. They were with some friends, enjoying our festival-tour.

I looked to see if she was still wearing her *heart*. I noted she was not.

I asked, "Where is your locket?"

She responded. "Oh, my mother is babysitting tonight."

THE PATRIOT INN'S FAVORITE RECIPES:

MOTHER'S JAM
Dedicated to my mother Helen Adamson Dodge

Boil together 2 to 3 minutes:
5 cups fresh or thawed frozen fruits
1 package of "Sure Jell" fruit pectin

Add
1 tablespoon of butter
7 cups of sugar

Boil for 3 minutes and dip a silver
spoon into the mixture. When it is done, the jam
will slide off the side of the spoon in sheets.

Pour into sterilized jelly jars. Place boiled flats and
rings on the jar opening. Tighten to seal.

Those that do not seal, I put in the freezer.

VERLE'S FRENCH CHOCOLATE

Put in a saucepan:
2 oz unsweetened chocolate
½ cup cold water

Stir over low heat until the chocolate melts.

Add
¾ c sugar
Dash of salt

Cook until thick (about 10 minutes).

Cool.

Fold in
½ cup heavy whipping cream

When ready to serve, heat:
1 qt milk

Pour hot milk into each cup.

Top with a tablespoonful of the chocolate mix.

Serves 6.

VERLE'S ORIGINAL CREPES

In medium bowl beat until thoroughly mixed:
1 Cup flour
4 eggs
¼ teaspoon of salt
1 teaspoon of sugar

Mix in:
1 Cup heavy whipping cream

Add to mixture:
1 teaspoon of vanilla

Grease a 7-8 inch crepe pan lightly. Heat over medium-high heat. A drop of water on the pan sizzles and bounces when it is ready. Pour about *3 tablespoons batter* into pan, tilting pan to spread evenly. When crepe is light brown and set, turn to brown other side. Remove from pan. Repeat, making approximately 14 crepes.

Serve with *a prepared fruit sauce or warmed maple syrup and butter.* Make *powdered sugar shaker* available.

(NOTE: can use *prepared pie fillings for filling: peach, apple, blueberry etc.* This mixture may be prepared two hours before use and refrigerated.)

FRENCH TOAST

Preheat griddle brushed with vegetable oil.

Set aside six slices of French bread, sliced thick.

Beat with a wire whisk:
3 eggs
½ cup of heavy whipping cream
1 teaspoon of vanilla
1/4 teaspoon of cinnamon
Dash of salt

Dip bread, coating each side, and fry until golden brown on both sides.

Shake *powdered sugar* over slices and serve with it *hot syrup and butter*.

Serves 6

ULLA'S OVEN PANCAKES:
By Ulla Geduldig Yatrofsky

Heat oven proof pan on top of a range and add:
2 tablespoons of butter, melt.

Beat:
2 eggs
1/2 cup flour

Add:
1/2 cup milk
a touch of nutmeg

Pour into an eight inch hot pan, bake 425° for
16 minutes until puffed and light golden brown.

Sprinkle with powdered sugar.

Serve immediately with fresh fruit or syrup
and whipped cream.

Note: This goes well with scrambled eggs and
fried bacon.

Syrup:

Melt: *2 tablespoons of butter* in a small skillet
over medium heat.
Add:
1 medium apple sliced
2 tablespoons of firmly packed brown sugar
1/4 cup maple flavored syrup
1/4 teaspoon cinnamon

Cook 4 to 5 minutes.

Keep warm.

Spoon over pancake and sprinkle with powdered sugar.

WAFFLES

Mix :
2 cups Bisquick
1 cup milk
½ cup heavy whipping cream
2 egg yolks separated

Set aside.
2 eggs whites separated and beaten
1 tsp. Vanilla

Fold into the mixture the beaten egg whites
and vanilla.

Bake in hot waffle iron until steaming stops, and
waffle is golden brown.

Serves 4

CRANBERRY OAT SCONES

1 1/2 cup flour
1 cup oatmeal
1/4 cup sugar
1 tablespoon baking powder

Mix all of the above and cut in *1/2 cup butter.*

Stir in :
1/2 cup dried cranberries or raisins
1/3 cup of milk and 1 egg blended.

Knead all 8 to 10 minutes

Make two balls pat to flatten on a greased cookie sheet.
Sprinkle with ¼ tsp. *cinnamon and 1 tblsp. sugar mix.*

Cut into wedges.

Bake at 400° for 12-15 minutes or until golden.

Cut into wedges. Serve with *clotted cream and lemon curd.*

Serves 6-8

FRENCH POACHED EGGS

Bring about *3 pints of water* to a full boil
in a deep saucepan.

Add:
1 Tbsp. Vinegar
½ Tbsp. Salt.

Break *one egg* into a saucer.

Stir the boiling water vigorously around and around
the edge of the pan with a wooden spoon held almost
upright. As soon as a well forms in the middle of the
water, stop stirring and slip the egg into the center of
the well. Lower the heat and cook until the white is
set. Take out with a skimmer.

Serve.

Repeat until the desired number of eggs is prepared.

Very attractive dish.

FRENCH SCRAMBLED EGGS

Whip:
6-8 eggs
1/2 cup heavy whipping cream

Add seasoning:
1/2 teaspoon of Tony Chachere's Creole seasoning

Preheat large frying pan with *1 tablespoon olive oil* and pour egg mixture into cook.

Do not over stir, just gently fold and stir until mixture is cooked thoroughly.

Top with *¾ cup cheese* and serve hot.

Note: we serve sausage pan fried with this or ham steak baked in the oven for 20 minutes at 375° topped with a cinnamon and sugar mixture.

SCRAMBLED EGGS CREOLE

Put in a skillet:

2 tbsp. Butter
1 slice onion diced.

Saute 5 minutes.

Add:
1 cup tomatoes
1 teaspoon Sugar
salt and pepper

Cook 5 minutes.

Add:
5 eggs, beaten slightly
¼ cup grated cheese (if desired).

Stir and cook until creamy.

Serves 4.

INDIVIDUAL QUICHE

Combine:
Three eggs
1/2 cup Bisquick
1/4 cup melted butter
1 1/2 cup of milk
Dash of pepper

Grease six ramekins.

Pour mixture into each one.

Top with:
3/4 cup shredded cheddar cheese
1/3 pound of fried sausage

Bake at 350°for 15 to 20 minutes or until knife comes out clean when inserted in center.

Serve while hot.

Note: sauteed onions and peppers can be added for a great taste.

Note: Other options include: ham instead of sausage with Swiss cheese, bacon and fresh cherry tomatoes, sliced apples, lump crab meat, and shaved Parmesan cheese.

FRENCH BAKED EGGS

Grease the number of ramekins you need for the number of guests plus extras, because many men will eat more than one.

Break *one egg* into each ramekin

Pour *1 tablespoon of heavy cream* over the egg

Shake *Tony Chachere's Creole seasoning* over each

Top with *a heaping tablespoon of four Italian cheeses.*

Bake at 375°for 15 minutes

Serve hot.

You can add crumbled bacon, cooked sausage, or chopped pieces of ham.

Note: when we used ramekins for individual servings we gave guests small pot holders to hold them so they could eat out of the dish or turn it out unto the dinner plate.

POTATOES AND KIEBALSA SAUSAGE

Saute' in one tablespoon of *olive oil.*
½ medium onion chopped
1 cup of a red, green and yellow peppers, chopped

Add the sausage and cook through:
One ring of kiebalsa sausage thin sliced crosswise.

Add and season with salt and pepper to taste.
Six large Yukon gold potatoes baked or boiled
cooled and sliced.

Note: I have used Creole, Italian, or French seasonings
for added flavor.

Serve hot with scrambled eggs.

Fry tomatoes and onions in olive oil as a side dish. Top
with four blended Italian cheeses.

PLANTATION HASH BROWN POTATOES

Beat together
4 eggs
½ cup heavy cream
Set aside

Fry:
Six to eight slices of bacon (I use *Pampered Chef*
oven stone-ware and fry the bacon in the oven at 375°)

Drain and save bacon grease. Crumble bacon.

Fry in bacon grease:
2 cups of Ore Ida O'Brien potatoes

Add:
½ fried bacon pieces to the potatoes.
Brown all.

Leave that mixture in the pan then pour over the top of
it the egg and cream mixture.

Lower the heat, leave covered, cook for 7 to 10 minutes
until done.

Top with rest of crumbled bacon and 1 cup sharp
cheddar cheese, and serve.

Serve with tomato salsa. I use mild Pace salsa with
fresh tomatoes chopped and stirred in, or chili sauce.

RON'S FRENCH OMELET

Note: The general rule is to never make an omelet with more than 4 eggs. Make several small ones instead.

Note: Select an omelet pan carefully. It is not necessary to keep a pan just for omelets, but the pan should be a heavy one. (Cast iron is excellent because it heats evenly). Keep the surface of the pan very smooth.

Beat slightly, just enough to blend the egg yolks
and whites:
4 eggs

Add:
¼ C. heavy cream
½ Tsp. Salt
1/8 Tsp. Pepper

Melt in hot omelet pan:
2 tablespoon butter

When the butter begins to sizzle tip the pan to make sure it spreads over the surface. Add the egg mixture and reduce the heat slightly. As the omelet cooks, lift it with a spatula, letting the uncooked part run under, until the whole is creamy. Increase the heat to brown very slightly underneath. A perfect omelet is creamy inside, or *Baveuse*.

Turn unto a hot platter and fold double. Serves 2 or 3.

VARIATIONS TO RON'S OMELET

Saute' in butter
1 tablespoon minced parsley or
2 tablespoon minced green or red peppers

Or:
Add to the eggs ¼ cup croutons

Or:
Add to the eggs ¼ cup grated cheese and cook
as above. (Gruyere cheese is especially good.)

Or:
Cut ¼ pound bacon into small squares. Fry until crisp
and brown. Drain off the fat and in it fry 1 cup ¼ inch
potato cubes until delicately brown. Drain and mix
with the bacon. Fold half into the Omelet and put the
rest around the edge.

Or
Omit the pepper. Add 1 ½ tablespoon very fine sugar
and ½ Tsp. Vanilla. Before folding, spread with jam,
tart jelly or marmalade. Sprinkle with sugar. As a
fancy touch, score with a hot skewer. Serve as dessert.

OMELET AUX FINES HERBES. Do original recipe ½
teaspoon each of finely cut chives, parsley, tarragon,
(or chervil), and watercress. Use any combination or
alone.

OMELET SOUBISE:
Turn the omelet out onto a ovenproof platter. Pour
Soubise Sauce (onion sauce) over the omelet. Sprinkle
with 2 tablespoon. Parmesan Cheese. Bake at 425
degrees until the cheese melts.

RON'S DELECTABLE FILLED OMELETS.

Before folding the omelet, spread with *2 Tbsp. Heavy sweet or sour cream, grated cheese, crumbled cooked bacon or chopped cooled sausage.*

Or:
Fill with any of the following, heated so that the omelet will not be cooled. *Cooked vegetables,* cut small and heated in butter. *Asparagus tips, peas and chopped spinach* are especially good.

Or:
Chicken or turkey, cooked, chopped, and creamed or seasoned.

Or:
Chicken livers, cooked, and minced.
Fish, cooked, flaked, or creamed.
Ham, cooked and ground fine, or ham spread.
Tuna cooked or canned, cut small and creamed or heated in butter
Mushrooms, creamed or sauteed,
Tomatoes, fresh or canned cut up and seasoned.

POTATO REFRIGERATOR ROLLS

Place in a small mixing bowl:
3/4 cup of warm water

Sprinkle *2 packages of dry yeast* in warm water
and let it stand until it forms a sponge on top.

Set aside

Mix flakes in hot water, let stand 5 minutes.
1/2 cup hot water
one cup of instant potato flakes

Stir into the softened potatoes:
2/3 cup sugar
1 1/2 teaspoon salt
2/3 cup lard or shortening

Add the yeast and warm water mixture

Stir in:
Two eggs beaten

Add:
4 1/2 -5 cups of sifted flour as is needed.

Then knead for 10 minutes.

Use *2 tablespoons of softened butter* to butter large
bowl

Place kneaded dough in buttered bowl and cover with
a damp cloth. Store in refrigerator up to five days.

This is the basic recipe for the following dinner bun
and cinnamon roll recipes.

158

Preheat oven to 400 degrees and bake 12-18 minutes or until golden brown.

VARIATIONS:

DINNER ROLLS:

Shape ½ dough into 12 oval balls, tapering ends slightly. With sharp floured knife slash lengthwise halfway through center of each roll.

Place 2 inches apart on greased cookie sheet. Cover let rise until doubled, about 30 minutes. Brush with *butter or egg glaze* and bake at 400° until golden brown.

Glaze: Beat *1 egg and 1 tablespoon of milk* until frothy.

CINNAMON ROLLS:

Grease well 13"x 9" baking pan.

In a small bowl, combine:
½ cup brown sugar
½ cup pecans, chopped
½ cup dark seedless raisins
½ tsp cinnamon.

Set aside.

Roll dough into 18"x 12".

Brush with:
¼ cup melted butter.

Sprinkle with above sugar mixture.

Starting as an 18" side, roll jelly roll fashion. Pinch seam to seal. With roll seam side down, cut dough crosswise into 15 slices. Place in oiled pan. Cover; let rise in a warm place until doubled about 40 minutes.

Bake at 400° for 25 minutes or lightly browned.

Cool slightly in pan on wire rack and apply glaze.

Glaze:
2 cups powdered sugar
½ teaspoon vanilla extract
3 tablespoons of warm water

Serves 15

LAZY MAPLE CRESCENT

Combine:
1/4 cup of butter
1/4 cup of brown sugar
2 tablespoons of maple flavored syrup

Place in 9 inch round cake pan then in oven
3 to 4 minutes or until butter melts.

Blend well and sprinkle with:
1/4 cup of coarsely chopped pecans

Set aside.

Without unrolling cut each roll into six slices:
8-oz crescent rolls

In a small bowl combine:
1 tablespoon of sugar
1/2 teaspoon of cinnamon

Dip sides of the rolls into the sugar and
cinnamon mixture and arrange slices
in pan.

Sprinkle remaining sugar.

Bake at 375° for 17 to 20 minutes.

Cool 1 minute invert into a serving plate

RUTH'S SPONGE CAKE
By Ruth Schnabel

Whip a minimum of 5 minutes- beat until thick
light yellow:
6 eggs

Add:
1/2 cup sugar

Beat until thick and creamy -one additional minute

Fold into mixture:
1 cup flour

Pour in paper lined tart pans.

Bake at 350° for 20-25 minutes

Free bottom of small cakes and lift out.

Top with sliced strawberries and blueberries mixed
with *1 cup sugar*.

Top with whipped cream.

Can use canned fruit pie fillings and top with
whipped cream.

JANE'S SOUR CREAM COFFEE CAKE

Mix together:
One box a white cake mix.
½ cup sugar
¾ cup of vegetable oil
1 cup sour cream

Beat well.

Add *4 eggs* one at a time, beating well after each addition.

Grease and flour a bundt pan.

Pour in half of batter.

Mix:
4 tablespoons of brown sugar
2 teaspoons cinnamon

Sprinkle 1/2 filling over batter. Blend rest in swirls in last half of batter.

Bake 325° for 1 hour. Cool 10 minutes and remove.

Mix glaze:
1 cup of powdered sugar
2 tablespoons of milk.

Spread glaze over cake.

COFFEE CAKE

Cream together until fluffy:
¾ cup butter (1½ stick)
1 cup sugar

Add while mixing:
2 eggs (one at a time)

Thoroughly mix and put to the side.

In another bowl mix together:
2 cups flour
1 teaspoon baking powder
¼ teaspoon salt
1 ¼ teaspoon baking soda

Add this mixture to the egg mixture

Add:
1 cup sour cream.

Set this mixture aside.

In a medium-small bowl, mix:
¼ cup white sugar
1/3 cup brown sugar,
2 teaspoon cinnamon
½ cup finely chopped pecans or walnuts.

Swirl this mixture into the cake batter above.

Pour batter into a 9"x13" greased cake pan.

Bake at 350° for 35 minutes.

ICING FOR CAKE:

Beat together well:
1- 8oz.pkg. cream cheese
1 pound box of powdered sugar
½ cup butter (1 stick)
1 cup chopped walnuts,
1 teaspoon vanilla
If it seems dry add a few drops of warm water.

This is more than needed to frost one cake.

Left over icing can be stored for a month.

BRAN MUFFINS

Mix dry ingredients:

1-15 ounce box of raisin bran (8 cups)
5 cups flour
3 cups sugar
5 teaspoons of soda
2 teaspoons salt

Add liquid ingredients, mix together:
1 cup vegetable oil
One quart of buttermilk
Four eggs well beaten

Store in a five quart container and bake in muffin tins lined with paper liners as needed at 350° 12 to 20 minutes. Keeps for six weeks in fridge.

Note: can add dried cranberries and nuts.

PEANUT BLOSSOMS

Makes three dozen

Cream:
1/2 cup of shortening
1/2 cup of the peanut butter

Add and cream
1/2 cup of sugar
1/2 cup of brown sugar

Blend and beat well
1 egg
1 teaspoon of vanilla

Sift and mix
1 3/4 cup of flour
1 teaspoon of soda
1/2 teaspoon of salt

Chocolate candy stars

Shape 1 inch balls, roll balls in sugar, and place
on greased baking pan.

Bake at 375°for 10 minutes

Remove from oven top with *candy star*. Press star
firmly so cookie cracks around the edge.

Return to oven and bake 2 to 5 minutes

SUGAR COOKIES

Cream:
1 cup of butter
1 cup of Crisco
1 cup of powdered sugar
1 cup of white sugar
2 eggs

Add:
4 cups of flour
1 teaspoon of cream of tartar
1 teaspoon of soda
1 1/2 teaspoon of vanilla

Roll out using *powdered sugar* instead of flour.

Cut with cutters dipped in *powdered sugar.*

Place on cookie sheets and Bake at 375°
15-20 minutes or until lightly browned on edges.

NO BAKE COOKIES

Boil 1 minute and stir constantly:
1/2 cup of butter
1/2 cup of milk
2 cups of white sugar

Add and mix:
2 tablespoons of cocoa
2 teaspoons of vanilla
1/2 cup of peanut butter
2 1/2 cups of oatmeal

Shape them any way you desire them.

Lay them out on waxed paper.

CHOCOLATE CHIP COOKIES

Cream:
2 cups of butter
2 cups of brown sugar
2 cups of sugar

Add:
4 eggs
2 teaspoons of vanilla extract

Mix with:
4 cups of flour
5 cups of blended oatmeal
1 teaspoon of salt
2 teaspoons of baking soda
2 teaspoons of baking powder

Add:
8 ounces of chopped nuts
24 ounces of chocolate chips

Place on cookie sheets and bake at 375° 15-20 minutes or until lightly browned.

EASY -YUMMY BROWNIES

Bake brownies according to pkg. *Pillsbury Brownies.*

Remove from oven and immediately spread miniature marshmallows on top of the hot brownies.

Let set 2-3 Minutes

Spread with frosting.

CHOCOLATE FROSTING:

Boil together:for 1-2 minutes
1 cup sugar
6 tablespoon. milk
6 tablespoon butter

Stir in:
1 ½ cup milk chocolate chips

Beat until smooth and drizzle over brownies.

Work quickly as the frosting gets thick fast.

FRUIT AT THE PATRIOT INN

1. Spring and Summer:

Blueberries and sliced strawberries:
sprinkle with sugar*, mix gently, and serve in
stemmed sherbet dishes.

◴ *Our sugar is in a container with vanilla beans
which infuses the sugar with vanilla.

2. Summer Fruits

Cantaloupe, kiwi, watermelon, grapes, and
pineapple tossed lightly with sweetened orange juices
or apricot brandy. (Some of these we served alone.)

3. Fall and Winter Fruits

Canned fruits in glass jars by Del Monte such as
mandarin oranges, pineapple, and mixed fruit.
Sometimes we swould slice pears, apples, bananas or
grapes and mix with one of the canned fruits.

THE PATRIOT INN FRUIT CRISP

FEATURED IN A COOKBOOK:

[Note:*"This delicious treat was received from co-innkeeper, Ella Verle Weiss, who is also a member of the Fort Nelson Chapter of the Virginia DAR. The innkeeper noted that they have many military guests at the Patriot Inn and that men often ask for this recipe for their wives. And in truth, many women will call for the recipe."* Celebrate Virginia Cookbook © 2003 Rowena Fullinwider.]

Preheat the oven to 375°

Peel, core, and slice *5 large cooking apples.*

Arrange the apple slices in an 8 or 9 inch square pan.

Sprinkle with *1 tablespoon water.*

Combine in a large bowl and mix well:
¼ C. firmly packed brown sugar,
½ C all-purpose flour
¾ cup rolled oats,
1 Tsp. Cinnamon

Cut into this mixture with a pastry cutter
until the mixture is crumbly.
½ cup (1 stick) chilled butter

Sprinkle the mixture over the apples.

Bake at 375°for 40-45 minutes or until the apples are tender.

For an added twist, substitute peaches or pears for the apples. Serve warm with cinnamon-flavored whipping cream or top with whipped topping and sprinkle with cinnamon. As a breakfast treat, serve in individual ramekins.

Makes 6 servings.

VIRGIE'S PLUM CORDIAL

My sister, Virgie makes her cordial in beautiful bottles and gives them to family and friends.

Fill:
1 quart jar half full with ripe wild sugar plums,
(Pierce each plum with several holes or slits.)

Add:
1 cup sugar per quart.

Fill jar with *vodka.*

Blue plums and elderberries can be used.

Store about 30-60 days.

Serve after straining or serve from bottle as is.

This is not only delicious but is beautiful on counter tops or in cabinets.

SPICED CRAB APPLES

Place in saucepan
1 cup sugar
2 cup boiling water
24 whole cloves
6 Allspice berries
1 (2") stick of cinnamon
A dash of salt.
Add 1 lb. crab apples

Simmer gently until the apples are tender. Skim out the fruit and pour a little of the juice over it. It it is to be stored overnight, cover with the juice and drain off most of it when you serve the fruit.

Serve with ham or pork.

Spiced cranberries or carrots can be created by substituting *raw cranberries or tiny new carrots* to the syrup in place of crab apples.

Spiced apricots or peaches. *Pour the syrup over cooked or canned pitted apricots or peach halves.* Do not cook, but let stand until the syrup is cold.

SAUTEED APPLES

Core *tart apples*. Pare if the skins are very tough.

Cut in ½ inch slices.

Saute' in butter or in bacon or sausage fat until just barely tender.

Turn with a broad spatula.

When the apples are nearly tender, sprinkle lightly with *brown sugar or grated cheese*.

Cover and cook until the sugar and cheese melts.

Serve with pork.

GLAZED PINEAPPLE

Drain *canned pineapple slices*.

Put in a single layer in a shallow baking pan.

Place over very slow heat or in a 250 degree oven.

Cook until the pineapple is almost transparent (2-3 hrs).

Garnish each slice with a *candied cherry*.

For pork.

RON'S FRUIT KABOBS

Men, this is great for outside grilling!

Push on skewers: *pineapple cubes, spiced apricot or peach halves, and cooked and pitted prunes.*

Brush with *butter* and grill (or broil) 5 minutes.

Serve hot with lamb chops or chicken.

FROZEN FRUIT DESSERT
(serves 24-30)

Mix in the large bowl:
1 large can of cut up apricots drained
1 can crushed pineapple (2 cups and Juice)
2-10 oz. frozen strawberries or raspberries,
(juice and all)
4 sliced bananas
Set aside

Boil for 3 minutes:
1 cup of sugar
1 cup of water
Cool

Pour cooled syrups over fruits and put into paper lined muffin tins and freeze.

When ready to serve take out of freezer fifteen minutes to allow a slight thawing. Serve in sherbet dishes.

MELON SUPREME

Cut melons in balls with a melon ball cutter. Combine more than one kind of melon or just use one. Sprinkle with sugar and rum or maraschino.

Serve in chilled shertet dishes.

BLUEBERRY SAUCE

Cook until bubbles:
4 cups frozen blueberries or other fruit (two 10 oz. pkg.)
2 tablespoons lemon juice
1/3 cup sugar

To the side, mix in small container:
 2 tablespoons of cornstarch
 2 teaspoons of water

 Add this mix to the boiling fruit mixture.

Serve in tall stemmed glasses:
1/2 cup yogurt
1/2 cup granola
1/2 cup yogurt

Top with blueberry or other fruit sauce.

HELEN'S HOLLANDAISE SAUCE

Beat until thick and set aside:
2 *egg yolks*

Heat in a double boiler top:
¾ cup water
2 tablespoon lemon juice
¼ teaspoon salt

Stir together until smooth
2 tablespoon cornstarch
¼ cup water

Add to the first mixture and stir to mix well. Pour slowly over the egg yolks, stirring constantly. Pour back into the double boiler top and set over hot water.

Add:
2 tablespoon butter

Cook and stir until thick. Makes about 1 cup.

WELSH RABBIT

Put in a double boiler or chafing dish or in a pan
 over low heat:

½ pound cheese of the best quality, cut small
1 tablespoon butter
¼ teaspoon salt
½ teaspoon dry mustard
Few grains cayenne or 1 teaspoon paprika

Cook slowly until the cheese melts, stirring occasionally.

Add
½ cup cream or milk
1 egg, slightly beaten

Stir constantly until thick.

Taste and add more seasoning if you like,
such as a few drops of *worcestershire sauce.*

Pour over saltines, toast, or broiled tomato slices.

Serves 4.

Substitute ale or beer for cream or milk.

Can also be spooned over:

Cooked broccoli, cauliflower, or asparagus on toast
or on sliced ham

Cooked chicken or turkey breast on buttered toast.
Top with bacon and set under broiler until
the bacon crisps.

Cooked lobster, shrimp, crab meat or tuna on rice or toast.

Slices of tomato on toast.

Sliced hard-cooked eggs or poached eggs on toast.

Toast spread with deviled ham.

DIP/ PEANUT SAUCE

Mix equal parts:
Mayonnaise
Honey
Peanut butter

Serve sauce with fruits or vegetable.

CHEESE SPREAD

Mix:
2 cups of grated sharp cheddar cheese
2- 3 tablespoons of pimento with juice
2 tablespoons of finely chopped onion
2 teaspoons of worcestershire sauce
1 tablespoon of lemon juice
Dash of salt
Dash of pepper

Add enough *real mayanaise* to moisten and spread.

Serve with crackers and celery.

I use this with toasted BLT sandwiches which
can be layered, toasted, or grilled.

Note: This is similar to the sandwich spread
Dana and I would eat at the Jefferson Hotel,
Richmond Virginia.

GRANOLA MIX

Mix:
4 1/2 cup of oatmeal
2 cups of shredded coconut
3/4 cups of brown sugar
1 cup chopped pecans
¾ cup sliced cup almonds

Mix, heat, pour over above mixture:
3/8 cup honey
1/4 cup vegetable oil

Stir frequently bake 20 minutes at 350°
in a 9"x13"x2" pan until coconut and almonds
are browned.

Cool:
1/2 cup raisins
1/2 cup dried cranberry
1/2 cup dried cherries

Stir in with above heated mixture.

MAPLE PECAN GRANOLA

Mix:
3 cups of rolled oats
1 cup chopped pecans
1 1/2 teaspoon of cinnamon
1/4 teaspoon nutmeg
1/4 teaspoon sea salt
Mix in pour over the above:
1 cup maple syrup
1 teaspoon vanilla extract
3 tablespoons of canola oil

Put on well oiled baking sheet
Bake 15 minutes at 325°
Stir and bake 10 more minutes.

PORTSMOUTH CITY HISTORY

VIRGINIA-A Guide to the Old Dominion.
Written and copyrighted by Virginia Writer's Project
Sponsored in part by the Work
Projects Administration, published in 1946.

The palisaded village of the Chesapeake Indians had long disappeared when Captain William Carver, mariner, acquired a plantation in 1664 along the brackish southern banks of the Elizabeth River. Later, despite the high offices he held, Captain Carver, "deciding to risk his old bones against the Indian rogues," participated in Bacon's Rebellion (1676) even attempting to capture Governor Berkeley. For this treasonable escapade, he was afterward hanged. His confiscated land was granted in 1716 to Colonel William Crawford, who in 1750 "laid out a parcel of land....into one hundred and twenty-two plots, commodious streets, places for a court house, market, and public landings for a town...and made a sale...to diverse persons...desirous to settle and build thereon speedily." Naming the place Portsmouth, he presented it to Norfolk County. In 1752 the general assembly "enacted...that the said...parcel of land be..established a town..and retain the name of Portsmouth."

Among the traders, merchants, and shipbuilders, chiefly Scots, who flocked to the new town, was Andre Sprowie. Acquiring land immediately to the south, he started the village of Gosport,named after the town opposite Portsmouth, England-by building a marine yard and tenements for workers. The British Government, recognizing the value of this enterprise, soon took over the yard as a repair station and appointed Andre Spowie nave agent.

When royal government ended in Virginia in 1775,

Governor Dunmore fled to Sprowle's home in Gosport, where he lived "Riotously upon his friend." For several months, he rallied Tories and Negroes about him and plundered the countryside, until his defeat at Great Bridge. Immediately afterward he joined the British fleet, accompanied by Sprowie.

Following the burning of Norfolk in 1776, Dunmore and his Tories took possession of Portsmouth and remained until the eccentric General Charles Lee arrived with his forces,and Dunmore sailed away with his whole following. Finding the town a hotbed of Tories, General Lee, "To quell this Tory-ism," had the houses "of the most notorious traitors" demolished. Sprowle's property and the abandoned marine yard were seized. Later, Fort Nelson, Named for General Thomas Nelson, was erected on Windmill Point.

One May morning 1779, a great gray British fleet, carrying two thousand men and commanded by Sir George Collier, anchored in Elizabeth River. General Edward Matthew of the fleet burned Fort Nelson and the marine yard, and the British departed. Portsmouth was the landing place and base for three other invading British expeditions under Leslie, Arnold, and Phillips.

The Revolution had repercussions in Portsmouth. A decade later, the navy yard,which the state had retained, was lent to the Federal Government, Captain Richard Dale was placed in command and the keel of a frigate was laid. The Chesapeake, the first ship built by the Federal Government, was completed in 1799. In 1801 the Government purchased the Gosport Navy Yard (now Norfolk Navy Shipyard) for $12,000.00. In 1798 a visitor remarked that "one might walk from Portsmouth to Norfolk on the decks of the vessels at anchor."

In an attempt to take Portsmouth and the navy yard during the War of 1812, the British landed 2300 men at Port Norfolk(now a part of Portsmouth), but the guns of Fort Nelson and Fort Norfolk stopped the invasion. A fresh onslaught was made on sandy Craney Island, lined with redoubts. Approaching in barges, the British were met with a bombardment that sank several vessels and caused an immediate retreat.

After extending its town limits in 1811, Portsmouth witnessed the opening of the Dismal Swamp Canal in 1812 a "boat containing 10,000 shingles" being the first to pass over the mingled waters of Chesapeake Bay and Albemarle Sound. In 1821, the first horse boat ferry was built, the town was swept by a fire of incendiary origin, but it was soon rebuilt. The land on which Fort Nelson lay was augmented by a 61-acre tract in 1826, the old fort was demolished, and on its sight, a naval hospital was begun. The town's first railroad was chartered in 1834 and public schools were established in 1846.

During this period, Portsmouth attended its jockey, cricket, and quoit clubs; frequented racecourses; watched the launching of the Lady of the lake (1830), which "moved by its own steam'" and welcomed such visitors as Andrew Jackson (1833) and Henry Clay (1844). Yellow fever, brought by a ship to Portsmouth in 1855. Of the 4000 people who remained in the town during the epidemic, 1089 died. In 1858 Portsmouth was chartered as a city.

When Virginia seceded from the Union, the Gosport Navy Yard was evacuated and burned, after which, Virginia troops occupied the area. In May 1882 the Confederates burned the navy yard and evacuated the area. Then Federal forces moved in, established martial law in Portsmouth, and again took possession of the navy yard.

Another phase of Portsmouth commercial era began in 1837 with the completion of the Portsmouth and Roanoke Railroad. Subsequently this line was incorporated in the Virginia and Carolina Railroad, which in 1900 became the Seaboard Air Line Railway, with its coastal terminus at Portsmouth, Branches of two other railroads, the Atlantic Coast Line and the Southern, bring inland produce to the city. Since taking over the lines the lines of the Atlantic and Danville Railway in 1894, the Southern has built an elaborate system of freight piers on the Western Branch.

At the beginning of the Twentieth Century, Portsmouth started extending its wharves along the waterfront, and, as necessity demanded, demolished its old houses to make way for modern business establishments.

APPENDIX

10 FORMS FOR INNKEEPERS
Samples to help you create your own forms.

The Patriot Inn
Bed & Breakfast
History

Take a step back in time to a
1784 Colonial home offering all the
luxuries of today, while enjoying
the views of the Elizabeth River.

Innkeepers:
Ron & Verle Weiss

201 North Street
Portsmouth, VA 23704
Telephone: 757 - 391 - 0157
Cell: 757 - 761 - 1380
Fax: 757 - 391 - 9290
E-mail: weisspatriot @aol.com
Website: bbonline.com/va/patriot

FRONT OF BROCHURE

196

The Patriot Inn is an architectural gem built in 1784, located in the Olde Towne Portsmouth National Historic District. The busy Elizabeth River waterfront is reflected in the hand blown window panes, just as it has been for over 200 years. Shopping and antiquing on High Street are just a few steps away, as are the Portsmouth Naval Hospital, the Tidewater Yacht Marina, and Norfolk waterside ferry.

This Colonial, English half-basement with Federal influence, rests on foundations of another dwelling dating to 1772. According to official documents, Thorowgood Keeling, a first lieutenant in the Virginia Milita, built the current dwelling in 1784. The earliest known owner of this property was Reverend John Agnew, a Tory Chaplain, who was a colonist loyal to King George III.

The American Revolutionary War played an important role in molding the history of Olde Towne Portsmouth. General Cornwallis, whose headquarters were in Olde Towne Portsmouth, decided to relocate his troops to Yorktown and loaded them on boats in front of the Patriot Inn. During this time, General Charles Lee was in charge of the forces that burned this Tory home to the foundation as an example to colonists still loyal to the king.

The Patriot Inn has been owned by many people in the history of Portsmouth. Nathaniel Pead, a shoe merchant, owned the home from 1787 to 1827. Other noteworthy owners were: Claudis W. Murdaugh, judge of the Court of Hustings; John K. Gayle, a member of the State Legislature; and Aurthur Emmerson, clerk of the Court of Hustings.

As the exterior of the home reflects colonial architectural details, the interior is discreetly decorated offering interesting corners to relax and enjoy the tranquility that permeates this lovely old Inn. With the original heart of pine wood floors, the stately main staircase, and the wonderfully carved mantles, the Inn is filled with furnishings that enable guests to step back in time and experience the spirit of colonial America.

INSIDE BROCHURE

The
Patriot Inn
Bed & Breakfast

Ron & Verle Weiss
Innkeepers
201 North Street
Portsmouth, VA 23704
Telephone: (757) 391-0157
Cell Phone: (757) 761-1380
Fax: (757) 391-9290
weisspatriot@aol.com
www.bbonline.com/va/patriot

BUSINESS CARD

The
Patriot Inn
Bed & Breakfast

The
Patriot Inn
Bed & Breakfast

2 NOTE CARDS ON 1 PIECE OF CARD PAPER

Ron & Verle Weiss
Innkeepers
201 North Street
Portsmouth, VA 23704
Telephone: 757-391-0157
Fax: 757-391-9290
E-mail: weisspatriot@aol.com
Web Site: bbonline.com/va/patriot

The
Patriot Inn
Bed & Breakfast

GIFT CARD FRONT/BACK

200

A gift for_____

In the amount of: $_____

To be used at *The Patriot Inn*.

From_____

Enjoy a step back in time to a 1784 Colonial home offering all the luxuries of today, while enjoying spectacular views of the Elizabeth River.

For reservations and information, call 757-391-0157.

Expires:_____

GIFT CARD/ INSIDE

The Patriot Inn
Bed & Breakfast

Ron & Verle Weiss
Innkeepers
201 North Street
Portsmouth, Va 23704

RECEIVED FROM:

FOR:

LODGING

_____ NIGHTS@ _____ =

TAX

_____ NIGHTS@ _____ =

FOOD

_____ NIGHTS@ _____ =

TAX

_____ NIGHTS@ _____ =

DETAILS:

| NIGHT1 | NIGHT2 | NIGHT3 | NIGHT4 | NIGHT5 |

| NIGHT6 | NIGHT7 | NIGHT8 | NIGHT9 | NIGHT10 |

| NIGHT11 | NIGHT12 | NIGHT13 | NIGHT14 | NIGHT15 |

RON AND VERLE WEISS
INNKEEPERS

Telephone: (757) 391-0157
Fax: (757) 391-9290

E-mail: weisspatriot@aol.com
Website: bbonline.com/va/patriot

REIMBURSEMENT FORM

202

The
Patriot Inn
Bed & Breakfast

Ron & Verle Weiss
Innkeepers
201 North Street
Portsmouth, Va 23704

Telephone: (757) 391-0157
Fax: (757) 391-9290

E-mail: weisspatriot@aol.com
Website: bbonline.com/va/patriot

BUSINESS LETTER WITH LETTERHEAD

The Patriot Inn
Bed & Breakfast

Take a step back in time to a
1784 Colonial home offering all the
luxuries of today, while enjoying
the views of the Elizabeth River.

Innkeepers:
Ron & Verle Weiss

201 North Street
Portsmouth, VA 23704
Telephone: 757 - 891 - 0157
Cell: 757 - 761 - 1380
Fax: 757 - 891 - 9290
E-mail: weisspatriot @aol.com
Website: bbonline.com/va/patriot

The Patriot Inn Bed & Breakfast
201 North Street
Portsmouth, VA 23704

BROCHURE FRONT & BACK

204

Patriot Inn Bed Chambers

General Charles Lee Bed Chamber

This bed chamber hugs the quiet North Street and conveys an old world charm.

- Four poster plantations, queen sized, antique bed with original wood burning fireplace flanked by two oversized wing chairs, and French armoire.
- Private bath with slipper tub, bidet, and antique French stand.

Marquis de Lafayette Bed Chamber

The historic charm of this bed chamber offers a cozy environment for the perfect escape.

- Rice-carved mahogany, queen sized, four poster bed with a wood burning fireplace.
- Private bath containing a whirlpool tub, two pedestal sinks with mirrored cupboards, and antique French stand.

Reverend John Agnew Bed Chamber

This bed chamber captures a warm atmosphere for a quiet slumber.

- Rice-carved mahogany, queen sized, four poster bed, antique French armoire, and two Martha Washington arm chairs.
- Private bath with a shower/tub and a sink set into a country French stand.

Commodore Richard Dale Bed Chamber

A snug nautically designed bed chamber offering a lovely view of the bustling Elizabeth River.

- Rice-carved mahogany, queen sized, four poster bed, antique English armoire, leather wing back chair, and ladder back side chair.
- Separate bath with walk-in shower and sink set into an antique cupboard.

Patriot Inn Policies

Room Rates: Ranging from $100 to $150 per night plus tax.

Payment: Cash, check, Visa, Master card, American Express, and traveler's checks.

Arrival/Departure Times:
Check-in after 2:00 p.m.
Check-out before 11:00 a.m.

Breakfast: English breakfast served at 8:00 or 9:00 a.m.

Open: All year round

Cable TV/VCR: Available in all rooms

Computer: wireless available

Restrictions: No pets, no children under 12, no smoking except fine cigars on the veranda overlooking the Elizabeth River.

Cancellations: Forty-eight hour notification is required or one-night accommodations will be billed.

"The Patriot captures the early American aspect of historic Olde Towne Portsmouth!"

BROCHURE INSIDE/ POLICIES

205

The Patriot Inn Reservation Request

1. Name:

2. Address:

3. Telephone Number:

4. Date of Arrival:
   Time of Arrival:

5. Date of Departure:
   Time of Departure:

6. Would you like to make a reservation?
   Type of payment?
   Credit card name and number:

7. Review Inn policies with customer...
   -cancellation (48 hrs notification required
      or 1 night accommodations)
   -restrictions (no pets, no children under 12, no smoking
   -check-in (after 2:00pm)
   -check-out (beofre 11::00am)
Notes:

PHONE RESERVATION FORM

ELLA VERLE WEISS

*V*erle lectured about La Fayette to Daughter's of the American Revolution chapters, Colonial Dames, and Daughters of the Colonists.

208

ABOUT THE AUTHORS

Head Innkeeper and author Ella Verle Weiss with her husband operated The Patriot Inn for twelve and a half years. Before that, she taught High School Physical Science, Interior design, and Family Consumer Science for 19 years. Also she was a part-time instructor of Nutrition, Anatomy, Physiology, and Chemistry at Western Iowa Tech Community College.

Verle was an assistant professor of Biology at Iowa Western Community College. She was president of the Iowa Community Colleges organization. She and her husband Ron co-chaired and organized the state-wide conference at Council Bluffs, Iowa for fifteen community colleges.

Verle received her Bachelor's degree at the University of Northern Colorado and her Master's degree at University of Nebraska.

She was a Staff Development Day presenter, and co-chair for the Procurement Community Black Tie Harvest Gala at Iowa Western Community College.

She was a honorary member and advisory of the Phi Theta Kappa. Verle was the Chair of various commissions. She received the Bellwether Award for her Phi Theta Kappa Chapter at the National convention at Anaheim, California. Verle was a Presenter of the Woman's Science Conference 1999. She was a member of the Torch Club and speaker. Verle is featured twice in *Who's Who Among America's Teachers:The Best Teachers In America Selected by the Best Students*.

Her fine art abilities complemented her scholastic ability. She developed her oil painting skills under the tutelage of Robert Lemasters at the Beasley Center at Portsmouth, Virginia. She is studying advanced drawing under Al Staszesky. She began her drawing instruction under Nicole Webber at TCC. She was a member of and a chairperson of the Museum and the Fine Arts Commission at Portsmouth for 6 years. Verle has been successful at displaying her artwork and marketing them.

She became enamored with the story of Lafayette because it was the time frame that a Tory family owned the Inn. She studied his life from many historical accounts and numerous visits to France. Out of these studies Verle developed a special knowledge of Lafayette. She is a member of the Fort Nelson Chapter Daughters of the American Revolution, Portsmouth, Virginia.

Innkeeper and co-author Ronald D. Weiss taught eight years as Biology Assistant Professor at Iowa Western Community College. Ron taught Microbiology, Biology, Environmental Science, and Survey of Biochemistry.Ron received his bachelors degree from Iowa State University and his masters degree at the University of Nebraska.

Ron was the president of the college Senate. He negotiated an open door policy in microbiology departments between Iowa Western Community College and Iowa State University. Ron was an instructor at Western Iowa Tech. Ron taught there full time for three years. Previous to that he taught high school. His classes won many awards in both Science, Parliamentary Procedure, and Vocational Agriculture.

Ronald is featured in *Who's Who Among America's Teachers:The Best Teachers In America Selected by the Best Students*. His name is also in the 2009 *Who's Who in America*.

ABOUT THE AUTHORS

Ron taught and tutored Biology at Tidewater Community College at Norfolk, Virginia for eight years. He was a member and speaker at the Torch Club, Portsmouth, Virginia.

Ronald D. Weiss excelled at sales as well as teaching. He spent six years as a territorial manager of Cargill Seeds. He was a Sergeant E-5 for six years in the Army Reserves.

Ron and Verle consider Christianity as an important part in their life and attend church regularly. They successfully raised a wonderful family.

Ron and Verle have traveled numerous times to Europe to visit Ron's families in France, and friends in Germany.

www.ingramcontent.com/pod-product-compliance
Lightning Source LLC
Chambersburg PA
CBHW072306210326
41519CB00057B/2813